KIDNAPPED BY THE VATICAN?

VITTORIO MESSORI

KIDNAPPED BY THE VATICAN?

The Unpublished Memoirs of Edgardo Mortara

Translated by Michael J. Miller

Foreword by Roy Schoeman

IGNATIUS PRESS   SAN FRANCISCO

Original Italian edition:
"*Io, il bambino ebreo rapito da Pio IX*":
Il Memoriale inedito del protagonista del "caso Mortara"
© 2005 by Arnoldo Mondadori Editore, Milan, Italy
© 2015 by Mondadori Libri, Milan, Italy

The memoirs of Father Edgardo Mortara were originally written in Spanish but were never published. An Italian translation of them by Andrea Vannicelli, which was approved by the author, is the basis of the English translation in this volume.

Cover photograph of Edgardo Mortara
Courtesy of Archivio dei Canonici Regolari Lateranensi

Cover design by Enrique Javier Aguilar Pinto

© 2017 by Ignatius Press, San Francisco
All rights reserved
ISBN 978-1-62164-198-8
Library of Congress Control Number 2017938952
Printed in the United States of America ∞

CONTENTS

FOREWORD

Why was the Mortara case such a cause célèbre in the second half of the nineteenth century, and why did it remain so controversial that it was the primary objection to the recent beatification of Pope Pius IX, almost a century and a half later? The case sits at the crossroads of the greatest social transformation of modern times: from a fundamentally religious view of the world to a fundamentally materialistic one. Those two views can lead to diametrically opposed conclusions about the Mortara case.

Promoting the welfare of its citizens has always been seen as a legitimate concern of the state, perhaps the primary one. Throughout the United States and Europe today, the state is considered to have the right even to remove a child from his parents to protect the child's physical and emotional well-being; this has been done in situations in which the child was deprived of proper medical care, left unattended in a parked car, allowed to play unwatched in a public park, or even subjected to secondhand smoke. Although people differ on the merits of particular cases, by and large we accept the principle that at some point the welfare of the child justifies the state's intervening and overriding the parents' right to care for the child—but only temporal, not eternal, welfare is usually considered.

But what if the teaching of the Catholic Church is true? What if, once created, the human person lives for all eternity, and the nature of that eternity—whether perfect bliss or unending misery—is dependent on the sacraments and on the person's moral formation? Then should not the same principle that gives the state the right to intervene for the physical welfare of the child give the state the right, perhaps even the duty, to intervene for the eternal welfare of the child as well?

That is the issue at the heart of the Mortara controversy. The Mortara case occurred when the fundamental notion of the state was undergoing a transition away from that of the "confessional" state—one in which there is an official state religion and the rights of other religions, if tolerated at all, are restricted. Throughout the nineteenth century and into the twentieth, popes consistently defended the confessional state against the encroachment of an increasing "separation of Church and State".[1]

The Mortara case emerged not only at the height of this philosophical shift in the idea of the state but also amid the violent transformation of Italy from a number of independent states, including the Papal States under the pope's direct rule, to a single unified state. Although the motivation of the Risorgimento was in part nationalistic, it was also heavily influenced by strongly anti-Catholic, anticlerical, antipapal forces.

In fact, much of the political reformation of Europe following the misnamed Enlightenment can be seen as a geopolitical manifestation of the rejection of Christianity, God, and religion that saw its first brutal expression in the homicidal, anti-Church French Revolution and continued in the atheistic communist revolutions that have plagued the world since the start of the twentieth century.

[1] See Gregory XVI, Encyclical *Mirari vos*, August 15, 1832; Pius IX, Encyclical *Quanta cura* and *The Syllabus of Errors*, December 8, 1864; Leo XIII, Encyclicals *Immortale dei*, November 1, 1885, and *Libertas praestantissimum*, June 20, 1888; Pius X, Encyclical *Vehementer nos*, February 11, 1906; and Pius XI, Encyclicals *Quas primas*, December 11, 1925, and *Casti Connubi*, December 31, 1930.

Many of the conflicts in twentieth-century Europe can be better understood in terms of atheism's battle against the Church than in terms of competing ethnic or national interests. The rise of fascism in Europe is directly linked to this battle, for the major figures associated with fascism in Europe—Franco, Mussolini, and Hitler—in their ascents to power, all presented themselves as defenders of the Christian state against atheistic communism.

The Mortara case arose in the center of this "perfect storm" of social and political turmoil. In addition to the Risorgimento in Italy, revolts against the confessional state were occurring or were soon to occur throughout Europe, as the "shackles" of Christendom were thrown off in favor of materialistic secularism in France, England, Spain, and Germany—and, of course, in Holy Mother Russia.

Into that battle waded, unknowingly, an innocent six-year-old boy, a Catholic nursemaid, and a pope of uncompromising integrity and courage. The result was the Mortara affair. Pope Pius IX stood as a bulwark against this secularizing trend that was transforming Italy and all Europe. The Mortara case provided an ideal opportunity for his opponents to attack him personally, as well as the authority of the Church and the very idea of a confessional state. For one's view of the morality of his actions depends on one's acceptance, or rejection, of the truths of the Catholic faith. In the light of the faith, what the pope did can be seen as not only legally justified but also morally justified; in the darkness of a total rejection of the faith, it appears unconscionable.

The circumstances of the case are straightforward. At the time of the incident, the Mortara family resided in Bologna, within the Papal States that were under the rule of Pope Pius IX. Contrary to the law at the time, the Jewish family employed a Catholic nursemaid, who surreptitiously baptized the infant Edgardo when he was at the point of death. The infant unexpectedly recovered; later, when the circumstances became known, the Mortara family was informed that since Edgardo was now a baptized Catholic, they would have to give him a Catholic education, as the law in the Papal States required for all Catholic children. Pressured by anticlerical forces, the parents steadfastly refused, requiring the pope to remove the child from his family in order to provide that Catholic education.

If one rejects the objective truth of the Catholic faith, then the Catholic confessional state, represented by Pope Pius IX as ruler of the Papal States, had no right to "impose its beliefs" and remove a surreptitiously baptized child from the care of his Jewish parents in order to assure him a Christian education. If, however, one accepts the teachings of the Church about the effects of the sacraments and the conditions for eternal salvation, might one not conclude that the pope had not only the right, but also the duty, to do as he did? Should the pope have put greater weight on the considerations in favor of the parents, or on the eternal salvation of the Christian child's soul? Whichever decision he made, one day he would have to answer for it before God.

Coming as it did at the very end of the existence of the Papal States and at the time of the emergence of increasingly successful anti-Catholic and anticlerical forces trying to remove all trace of "Christ" from "Christendom" and of "Holy Roman" from "Holy Roman Empire", the case drew down upon itself all of the passion and fury of that conflict. In the words of Pius IX, "All the governments of the Old and the New World united and conspired to take away from me, from Christ, and from His Church, the soul of this child.... I do not feel sorry, though, for what I have done on his behalf, to save a soul that cost the blood of God. On the contrary, I ratify and confirm everything." And what was Edgardo's view of the pope's decision? In his memoirs, he wrote "The angelic, admirable, immortal Pontiff ... was far above the frothing, angry waves of the human passions that conspired with Hell to wage a war without quarter against the Church of Christ.... He was as great as his magnanimous heart, as fearless and invincible as the Lion of Judah."

Here, to help resolve the debate, we have those memoirs published for the first time in English: the patient, loving, faith-filled testimony of Edgardo Mortara himself. In this account, brimming over with filial love and gratitude to Pope Pius IX for fathering him into eternal life, after his Jewish father had fathered him into physical life, Edgardo pours the soothing balm of love and truth over the turbulent waters of polemics, showing more eloquently than any argument could where the rights and wrongs of the case truly lie.

Roy Schoeman
June 11, 2017
Feast of Saint Barnabas

THE MORTARA CASE

By Vittorio Messori

When I was adopted by Pius IX, the whole world shouted that I was a victim, a martyr of the Jesuits. But in spite of all this, I, most grateful to Divine Providence, which had led me to the true Family of Christ, was living happily at Saint Peter in Chains, and in my humble person the law of the Church was in effect, despite Emperor Napoleon III, Cavour, and some other great men of this earth. What is left of all that? Only the heroic *"non possumus"* of the great Pope of the Immaculate Conception.

—Pio Maria Edgardo Mortara, C.R.L.

I am a Catholic on principle and by conviction, ready to respond to attacks and to defend even at the cost of my blood this Church you are battling.

I tell you that your words deeply offend my honor and my conscience and oblige me to protest publicly.

I am intimately convinced, by the whole life of my august Protector and Father, that the Servant of God Pius IX was a saint. And it is my conviction that one day he will be elevated, as he deserves, to the glory of the altars.

—Pio Maria Edgardo Mortara, C.R.L.

The first epigraph is from an 1893 speech given by Father Pio Maria Edgardo Mortara to the Catholic Conference in Würzburg, Germany. The Latin clause *non possumus* means "we cannot". The second epigraph is from Father Mortara's public protest against the French Chamber of Deputies, which in its July 7, 1879, session described him as a "victim of Pius IX and of clerical obscurantism". Count Cavour, Camillo Benso, was an Italian statesman.—Trans.

The memoir published here was written by Father Edgardo Mortara (his religious name was Pio Maria) in 1888, when he was thirty-seven years old and was in Spain for his apostolate—hence the choice of the Castilian language—and when he still had a good fifty-two years left before ending a fervent religious life.

His life was so edifying that his superiors in the order, after acknowledging the reputation of holiness that surrounded the deceased and the pilgrimage of the faithful to his tomb, decided to begin the process for his beatification. But the whirlwind of World War II upset these plans. There are some, however, who propose restarting the procedure so as to give the Church another saint who would be particularly important today, given his exemplary history.

The cleric died, just before turning ninety, on March 11, 1940, in the abbey of Bouhay in Belgium, a land that would be invaded by the Germans a few weeks later. Although the Church has always welcomed with open arms the Jews who asked to be a part of her, even considering them her favorite sons, the materialistic and pagan racism of National Socialism persecuted baptized Jews too, even if they had become religious. Such was the case with Edith Stein, snatched from her cloister and taken away to die in a concentration camp.

In his final years, Father Mortara expressed the desire to end his long life in his native Italy, which he dearly loved, even though he had had to flee from it to avoid the "liberation" that the Piedmontese tried to force on him when they entered Rome with guns blazing. His confreres, in 1939, therefore arranged for the transportation of the sick old man to one of their houses in Genoa, but the outbreak of hostilities thwarted this plan, too.

It is possible that the autobiography—which the cleric wrote in the third person—following these pages of our commentary was prepared to be read at the *Katholikentag*, the annual congress of the Catholics in Germany, whose language Father Mortara knew so well. He preached and wrote not only in Italian, but also in German and Spanish, in French, Latin, Greek, English, Hebrew, and even, of all things, in Basque, a non-Indo-European language notorious for its difficulty.

Thinking of translating it into German for the Catholic congress—in which he did not participate that year, however, but in 1893—Father Mortara wrote the memoir in Spanish so as to spread, beyond the Pyrenees also, accurate knowledge of his story, about which endless distortions and "black legends" had arisen. At the time, he was in Oñati, in the Basque Country, to build a new house for the Canons Regular, as well as a seminary and a shrine dedicated to the Sacred Heart, the most practiced devotion in a Church undergoing persecution and needing help from Heaven more than ever. In Paris, the famous, gigantic Sacré-Cœur Basilica was under construction on the hill of Montmartre, and in Italy, too, basilicas and shrines were going up in honor of that devotion.

Spain had to be up to the occasion, and Father Mortara had dedicated himself to this project. It was necessary, however, to collect many alms, and for this reason, too, that singular cleric, begging for the love of Christ, had to tell his story, which had caused much excitement and many conflicting emotions throughout the world.

Of that story, we recall only the main elements in this chapter. In the pages that follow, the protagonist himself recounts how things truly went: He was born to a family of modest Jewish merchants, in the second half of the nineteenth century in Bologna, which was the administrative center of a legation of the Papal States. He was baptized, furtively but validly—when a doctor had declared he was at the point of death—by a young maidservant who had been hired against the law designed to avoid such cases, which prohibited Jews from having Christian household help. The woman kept his Baptism secret for five years; then, in 1857, the news came to the attention of the local religious authorities, who immediately informed Rome. Finally, after months of discreet investigations, the decision—painful but necessary according to both canon law and civil law—was made by the pope himself, in June 1858, to proceed with the separation of the child from his family so as to raise him in a Catholic boarding school.

The Church has always forbidden the Baptism of Jewish children without their parents' consent. If it is validly administered, however, its effects are objective (*ex opere operato*) and permanent. Therefore, the new Christian must be educated as a Christian—at least until the age of majority, when he will be able to choose between persevering in the gospel faith and returning to the synagogue. On this matter, the Church has no choice (not even today, as we will see), if she is not to disown her entire sacramental theology; hence, the caution so that such cases would not occur; hence, the papal laws to avoid ill-advised acts by misguided Christians.

But then there arose the Mortaras' opposition to the transfer of their almost seven-year-old child to a Catholic institute right there in Bologna; the need for a police escort to Rome, and the affectionate interest of Pius IX, who immediately took the child under his personal protection; and finally, the start of the international "case", perpetuated not only by the Jewish communities but also by the liberal and Masonic press and by governments such as Cavour's. In his letters, Cavour said that he was quite glad about this confirmation that the temporal power of the Church was an anachronism, and he declared himself enthusiastic about an affair that was so helpful to his political plans. *La Civiltà Cattolica*, a daily newspaper founded only eight years earlier but already the unofficial mouthpiece of the Church, wrote that the child "stirred up a hornet's nest of declamations, of journalistic diatribes, of interventions by politicians that deafened the world". It was an uproar that, as we will see, is far from being quieted even today.

After that, however, there was the passage of eighty-two years in which the "unfortunate kidnapped child" studied, freely chose the priesthood and the religious life, fled to escape the liberals who wanted to "liberate" him, and dedicated himself to a life of fervent apostolic work, which concluded, finally, with an exemplary death. It was burdened by only one grief: that his prayers and powers of persuasion were not enough to induce anyone else in his family to accept the gospel.

For Mortara, telling how things really had happened was also, and perhaps most importantly, a duty of justice toward Pius IX, who had been attacked, vilified, and threatened because of the "abduction of the Jewish child" and who instead deserved a hymn of thanks, affection, and gratitude. The pope himself had told him many times, his voice breaking with emotion: "You have been for me the son of Providence, but also the son of tears."

It is no coincidence that the cleric decided to describe his work as follows on the first page of his autobiographical manuscript: "Historical notes accompanied by a forceful vindication of the great pope, of blessed and grateful memory, written by Father Pio Maria Mortara". Upon becoming a religious, he had decided to take the name of his spiritual father, adding to it the name of Maria, to whom he would always be extraordinarily devoted. Indeed, he would see a mysterious connection between his entrance into the Church, in 1858, and the apparitions in Lourdes, which happened in the same year. Through his initiative, at the monastery of Bouhay, where he later died, a full-scale replica of the grotto in Massabielle was built, and this shrine started in Belgium a pilgrimage that continues today.

On the morning of September 3, 2000, in a crowded, festive Saint Peter's Square, as we commented live for Italian television on the beatification of Pope Pius IX, the most beloved and hated pope of the last two centuries, the words that his spiritual son used to close his manuscript sounded prophetic:

> There will come a day, yes, and it is not far away, in which, once they have stopped listening to the calumnies and the "*Crucifige*" (shouts of "Crucify!") of the dregs of humanity, posterity will accept the poor arguments of the Mortara child, so as to tie them into scented garlands of immortal flowers that will adorn and decorate the altar on which the Catholic world will greet, with enthusiastic acclamations, PIUS IX, THE SAINT.

At the beginning of the twentieth century, during the canonical process for the beatification of this pope, Father Mortara was called to testify. His statements are summed up well by the final words of his deposition, which we add to those that we chose as a motto for our book:

> Every time I have returned to the Eternal City, with profound emotion I have prostrated myself on the tomb of my Venerable Father and Protector; my gratitude to him has no limits, and I will always consider him a wise and holy Pope. He, in his epitaph, invited worshippers to pray for him: *Orate pro eo*. I confess that, as often as I have read those words, I have said in my heart: *Sancte Pie, ora pro me!* [Saint Pius, pray for me!]

Presenting the truth about that pontiff, who reigned over the Church for almost thirty-two years—longer than any other pope besides Saint Peter—is particularly important for Catholics.

First of all, Pius IX is enrolled among the Blessed—a matter that in itself is already binding, given that the pope exercises his infallibility in proclaiming saints (and, according to some theologians, in declaring blesseds, too). To put it bluntly: the consequences would be disastrous if John Paul II had been wrong, as many shouted, in granting to his predecessor the glory of the altars. From a faith perspective, he cannot have erred in his judgment: hence, at least for believers, veneration is obligatory.

Secondly, Pius IX was also the pope who convened Vatican Council I, with the proclamation of the dogma of papal infallibility, the most disputed dogma even within the Church, to the point of causing the schism of the Old Catholics.

Disputed also was another dogma that Pius IX proclaimed, which after consultation with the bishops worldwide, settled a thousand-year debate: the dogma of the Immaculate Conception of Mary, which basically had always been believed by the Church but had never been defined ex cathedra. Heaven seemed to grant a unique, unprecedented privilege to this pope, a direct confirmation of a papal decision: four years after the proclamation of the dogma, Mary identified herself, in Lourdes, as the Immaculate Conception. Never was a pope confirmed so authoritatively!

Pius IX was also the one who encouraged Don Bosco and defended him against his opponents, allowing him to found the religious community—the Salesian Congregation—that in those years became the second largest in the Church, after the Jesuits. During his pontificate the largest number of congregations in history, both male and female, began, and the foreign missions flourished and expanded at an unprecedented rate.

Pius IX is the pope who, with his *Syllabus of Errors*, far from defending the past (as conformists believe or as the polemicists would have us think) showed, on the contrary, a truly prophetic vision, warning Catholics—but in vain—about the social and political ideologies that would devastate the twentieth century. Many—even among the clergy—pronounce the title of that encyclical with a shiver of horror, yet practically no one has read it. In reality it foresees and condemns in advance all the isms (scientism, laicism, materialism, racism, nationalism, socialism, fascism, communism, and so forth, in a dreadful litany) that would drench future decades with blood.

Telling the truth about Pius IX is therefore important, perhaps crucial, considering the relevance that his long, turbulent reign had for the Church. Hence, also, the timeliness of publishing this autobiography of Edgardo, who had become Father Mortara, which helps to clarify what for many people would be one of the darkest shadows—the brutal, cynical, inhuman abduction of a child!—on the white garment of the Vicar of Christ. At stake here also is the good name of John Paul II. The home page of the most popular Italian anticlerical website on the Internet lists some of the worst "Catholic infamies". Among them is the beatification of the "criminal pope", the one who snatched children from their mothers' arms. In glorifying this monster, Pope John Paul II allegedly revealed his own true nature.

The text we present here may have been made into a booklet and circulated in Spain (we do not know how widely); as far as we know, it was not translated into other languages and is not found in any bibliography. Around the 1930s an in-house edition of it was made, again in Spanish, intended for "internal use", which means it was only for the members of the order. It was entitled *El niño Mortara y Pio Nono* (The Mortara child and Pius IX), with an explanatory subheading that needs no translation: *Narración autógrafa del "Caso Mortara", escrita por el protagonista Rvdo P. Pío María Mortara, C.R.L.* This is the text, consisting of ninety pages in a small format, that we rediscovered in the Roman archive of the Canons Regular, at the famous Church of Saint Peter in Chains, nowadays besieged by tourists who are enthralled by Michelangelo's *Moses*.

In short, this text can be considered unpublished, because it never had graphic presentation or readership of a book, and it circulated only *pro manuscripto* in Spanish-speaking circles exclusively.

I suggested translating and publishing it, but not to cater to a few scholars, to satisfy the curiosity of some historian, or to please antiquarians. Thus these pages are not being marketed by a niche publishing house, but by the largest Italian publisher. One factor in the decision to make today's readers acquainted with the text, as I said, was the timeliness of reexamining an important aspect of the pontificate of Pius IX from an objective, nonsectarian perspective.

Then, too, there is no doubt that the "Mortara case" is still alive and of current interest. After about a century and a half from its beginning, it still occupies a place in our religious and cultural consciousness; it is often cited (but rarely studied) for polemical reasons and perhaps even with a partisan slant. As previously mentioned, for a long time an international campaign of defamation vehemently opposed the beatification of Pius IX. One Jewish-American organization went so far as to buy a whole page of the *Washington Post* for a plea in which they warned John Paul II not to glorify "the kidnapper pope".

Interfaith organizations declared that the Polish pope not only had not included, among his many requests for forgiveness, one for the "kidnapping" perpetrated by Pius IX but also was enrolling a sinister character among the Blessed. And this, they said, jeopardized the Jewish-Christian dialogue. Amos Luzzatto, president of the Union of Italian Jewish Communities, the day after he learned that John Paul II would beatify his predecessor during the Jubilee Year, issued an official statement:

> The involvement of Pius IX in a very painful episode for the Italian Jews, like the violent abduction of the child Edgardo Mortara from his Jewish family and his Catholic education to the point of making him a priest, left a memory of dark times of persecution in the middle of a century of emancipation. This wound has never healed, and Pius IX is undoubtedly for the Jewish communities a lamentable memory that has not been overcome.

Solicited by various parties, the grandnephews of Edgardo Mortara protested at the Holy See against that beatification and granted a series of interviews that were extremely polemical. This may be a repetition of what happened in 1858 and in the following years, when the family was convinced to adopt an uncompromising attitude, rejecting any mediation, by those who wanted to exploit the case and to amplify as much as possible what was presented as "an intolerable scandal" that required the immediate intervention of the "civil world" in order to demolish the power of the Vatican hydra.

The man who headed the Roman Jewish community in the nineteenth century, Sabatino Scazzocchio,

complained repeatedly about this interference by strangers, including powerful Jewish representatives from
around the world. The Jewish community of that time,
which for two thousand years had lived on the banks of
the Tiber (and which the popes, unlike other kings and
princes of Europe, had never banished), reacted harshly
when the liberal or Jewish press published news stories
like the one claiming that the child had been castrated, by
order of the "white-clad monster", so as to make him a
soprano for the Sistine Chapel!

Scazzocchio, to give just one example, wrote to the
boy's father, Salomone Levi Mortara, known as Momolo,
after his first visit to Rome to see his son and to beg for
his return through the support of his coreligionists in the
Lazio region:

> About Edgardo I am not able to tell you anything except
> that he is in perfect health. As for the case, I have no
> alternative but to repeat to you what Signor Alatri and all
> of us have said a thousand times by now: namely, that the
> indiscreet gossip of so many newspapers, which derive fuel
> for political passions from any event whatsoever, has poi-
> soned the matter. Whereas, if they had left it up to us to
> mind our own business, the legal line of conduct that has
> always been followed as our motto might have allowed us
> to attain our much-desired purpose, given the benign and
> charitable nature of him who is seated on high. Certainly
> it is not in these recriminations against journalism that she
> could find consolation for her immense sorrow, but I can-
> not help giving free vent to the words that cling to my
> soul, so as to water it with bitterness and anger.

David I. Kertzer, the American historian whom we will
soon meet because he is the author of a recent best seller
about the case that interests us, comments in dismay:

This is indeed a remarkable letter. The bitterness and anger of Scazzocchio, and perhaps that of the other leaders of the Roman Jewish community as well, were directed not against the Pope ... but at the liberal press that had championed the Mortara cause. Those who so loudly criticized the Church for taking Edgardo were denounced as self-seeking opportunists, more interested in making their own political points than in winning the child's release and the family's happiness.[1]

Kertzer claims to be surprised, even a bit indignant, because the head of the Jews in nineteenth-century Rome—in a private letter, thus above the suspicion of forced sycophancy—speaks about "the benign and charitable nature of him who is seated on high". The American historian comments, therefore, with bitter irony: "Only the lack of a capitalization in the last phrase makes it clear that the Jewish secretary is referring here not to the God of Abraham, Isaac, and Jacob but to Pope Pius IX."[2]

After so much work to demonize that pontiff, here is a Jew, a representative of all his confreres to boot, a Jew who had frequent personal contacts with Pius IX, who speaks well about him and with trust. On other occasions, too, the "pope's Jews" had disappointed historians with preconceived theses. For example (as Scazzocchio himself claimed in a meeting with him), they refused in 1849 to back the Roman Republic of Mazzini and Garibaldi. The community in the capital remained calm about it, did not comply with invitations to join the struggle, and even paid homage to the pontiff—who did not fail to commend it—when he returned from his Napoleonic exile.

---

[1] David I. Kertzer, *The Kidnapping of Edgardo Mortara* (New York: Alfred A. Knopf, 1997), 162–63.
[2] Ibid., 162.

Certainly, Rome was perhaps the only large city in the West (excluding Eastern Europe) that still had a ghetto, although it was mitigated to a great extent. But someone drew attention to the strange fact that, even though anyone could enter and leave the Papal States (which was anything but a police state: Massimo d'Azeglio and many other famous liberals, many foreigners among them, got along very well there, lamenting, if anything, the excessive affability of the authorities), even though the borders were therefore open, there was no emigration by the Roman Jews to the many countries where equal rights were already a reality. While entire boatloads of Russian Jews were taking refuge in America, while those under the Turkish yoke tried to leave, and from many European countries the "sons of Abraham" emigrated to the progressive capitals, Paris and London, practically no Roman Jew left the banks of the Tiber. Were they too poor to move? Apart from the fact that not all were, were there not even poorer ones who emigrated by steamship from Eastern Europe to the United States and, although in smaller numbers, to Brazil and Argentina? This is an aspect that no historian seems to have wanted to investigate. And yet, going beyond offenses and accusations, it could tell us much about the millennial coexistence of Jews and Catholics, of church and synagogue.

But let us return to the throbbing passion for obstruction before the beatification of Pius IX during the Jubilee Year. Naturally, one might question the appropriateness or even the legitimacy of such external intrusions into the activity of the Church, which follows her own laws and beliefs. It calls to mind the dry, realistic conclusion of a book that Giulio Andreotti dedicated, with love and admiration, to that pope: "Let everyone be resigned to the fact that Giovanni Maria Mastai Ferretti is being proclaimed blessed. And may they leave in peace those like me who admire him and pray to him!"

In any case the Church does not have to ask permission from the "world" to determine the criteria for proclaiming the sanctity of one of her sons. But today, as many have observed, Western culture has fallen under a new inquisition, under the harshly imposed and ruthlessly enforced dogmatism of political correctness, in which only one prejudice is allowed, albeit not encouraged—the one against Catholicism and, in particular, against those who, within it, seem to have overturned in the most intolerable way the tables of values of the New Pharisaism. Pius IX is one of those reprobates. And the Mortara case is one of his most unforgivable crimes.

The prevailing conformism requires, on the one hand, the demonizing of Pope Pius IX and, on the other, the exalting of Pope John XXIII, who is contrasted with his predecessors. This contrast would have aroused the indignation of John XXIII—not the mythical pope but the real one, who in calling the Second Vatican Council thought that it would last for a few months. In his mind this amount of time would have been enough to approve without delay the decrees already prepared by the Holy See. Once the votes were over, the council would be concluded on December 8, the feast of the Immaculate Conception, with the beatification by acclamation of Pius IX, of all people.

The "progressive" Pope John XXIII, in fact, had such great admiration for the figure of this "reactionary" predecessor that he showed impatience with the tedious formalities of the canonical process and wanted to have his venerated master brought to the honors of the altar by means of an extraordinary procedure. Indeed, one of his first telephone calls, on the day after his election, was to the postulator of Pius IX's cause, to find out how things were going. And his last outing in Rome, on the day before the conclave, was to San Lorenzo al Verano to recollect himself at the tomb of "his" Pius IX. The latter's baptismal name, Giovanni, is said to have inspired John XXIII's choice of his papal name. For this reason, too, many were not only unsurprised but also overjoyed that the two great popes were raised to the honors of the altar on the same day in 2000. Some no doubt smiled, with some bitterness, at the propaganda pitting the two popes against each other. It was Pope John's explicit intention that Vatican II should be the continuation and the conclusion of Vatican I, which Pope Pius IX had had to interrupt because of aggression by the House of Savoy.

There is another reason for the current relevance of the Mortara story. As I was writing these pages, in the winter of 2004–2005, a heated debate was being conducted in the mainstream media about the Jewish children who had been hidden in Catholic institutions during the Nazi occupation of Europe and had been baptized. Well, it was a rare speech then that did not refer to the Mortara case.

When John Paul II crossed the threshold of the major synagogue on the Tiber on April 13, 1986—and it was the first time for a pope—the president of the Union of Communities, on behalf of all Jews, cited this very controversy to deplore it, recalling how the memory of it has persisted.

If you type "Edgardo Mortara" into an Internet search engine, thousands of hits will appear in all languages, especially English since many in America have suddenly become passionate about the incident. If you go to the websites, you will discover that ardent emotions dominate discourse about the affair, which has become a polemical pawn and not the calm object of history.

To confirm this relevance it must be remembered that the major international best seller about the "case" is not a dusty, forgotten work from the 1800s: the heavy tome (almost five hundred pages) by David I. Kertzer appeared in the United States in 1996. In Italy it was immediately translated and published under the title *Prigioniero del papa re* (Prisoner of the Pope-King) by a large publishing house that prints mostly books for wide distribution.

The first Italian work with historical ambitions regarding the subject, even though it was marred by strong partisan passion, appeared in 1997. Its title is simply *Il caso Mortara*, with the subtitle *la vera storia del bambino ebreo rapito dal papa* (the true story of the Jewish child kidnapped by the pope). Its author is Daniele Scalise, a journalist who wrote the "Gaywatch" column for *Espresso* magazine from 2001 to 2002.

Hollywood has announced two film projects about the Mortara case with prestigious actors, and they are already in the works. Meanwhile, the theatrical production *L'affaire Mortara* was performed recently in Bologna by a famous company sponsored by the university there and the Teatro Stabile. This work is the latest descendent—so far—of a long tradition. Over the decades there have been countless theatrical works in many languages against various popes. One of them, *La tireuse de cartes* (*The Fortune-Teller*), had among the spectators at the premiere no less than French Emperor Napoleon III, who also intended to show thereby his disdain for all that had been done for him by the pope, whom he detested but was forced to protect militarily for political reasons.

And an odd, significant point by Antonio Gramsci, in the third volume of his *Prison Notebooks*, comes to mind: "It would be necessary to reconstruct the history of the

Mortara boy, which had such clamorous repercussions in the polemics against clericalism."

The relevance of the Mortara case lies also in its historical consequences, which continue down to our day. Just as the Dreyfus affair in the late nineteenth century was a powerful stimulus for nascent Zionism, the Mortara case brought about the foundation of the still-existing Alliance Israélite Universelle, the first Jewish organization of self-defense with a global perspective. This organization moved quickly and decisively, given that—in collaboration with *Archives Israélites*, one of the major Jewish newspapers—it offered a reward of 20,000 francs, a veritable fortune, to anyone who would organize an armed incursion into Rome to free the child from the clutches of his kidnapper. It would have been a violation of international law, but when it comes to the Catholic Church, subtlety was not and is not the order of the day. Anything was and is permitted against the "center of obscurantism".

In the United States, the 150,000 Jews who had already emigrated from Europe, especially from Eastern Europe, were still a scattered people; they did not form a homogeneous community but lived in groups that were often self-enclosed and scarcely connected with one another. Their reaction to the incident of the "little Jewish Italian boy snatched by the pope from his mother's arms", as it was reported extensively (with considerable melodrama) by the press, laid the initial organizational foundations of the Jewish-American community. In effect, the highly controversial Mortara case brought about the establishment of the Board of Delegates of American Israelites, which succeeded, among other things, in obtaining a federal law authorizing abstention from work on Saturday. The law was passed in the emotional wake of the incident. That child in Bologna was, in short, a powerful catalyst, a unifying factor that helped the Jewish world rediscover its common identity—both in the Old World and in the New.

And then, the Mortara case had a precise and important significance within the Risorgimento movement for Italian unification. It was, in fact, immediately used politically, with a determination that seems to border on cynicism. We will see this more clearly.

Again, with regard to historical repercussions: although the consequences of the case were serious for the ecclesiastical state and hastened its fall, Pius IX's firm stance against everything and everyone increased the opposition of his enemies but contributed mightily in the Catholic world to creating the image of the persecuted pontiff and giving him the aura of an intrepid *fidei defensor* (defender of the faith). All these things, reinforced then by his confinement to the Vatican behind the Porta Pia, created the image of the papacy that has come down to our day. Pius IX may have been the first pope whose portrait was hung even on the walls of shops and in the houses of the poor; if so, it was due to his resistance, which to some (starting with the "kidnapping") seemed truly heroic, against the aggression that he had to endure from the combined forces of Masonic lodges, secular governments, newspapers, and embassies.

The Mortara case is still relevant, because professional historians study it militantly and because it concerns the Church, albeit in its consequences. It is therefore—it bears repeating—a case that is often manipulated and used as a weapon in anti-Catholic polemics.

Here is just one example, chosen from among the most recent. In the debate over Jewish children taken in by the Church during the Holocaust, Sergio Minerbi, former Israeli ambassador to Brussels, spoke up. This well-educated, responsible man, and furthermore an Italian Jew—and as such, one might presume, better informed than others about an Italian incident, even though it later took on global dimensions—wrote about the case in an article for *Il Giornale* (January 6, 2005). Minerbi summed up the case as follows: "In 1858 a Jewish boy, Mortara, was kidnapped from his family in Bologna and baptized so as to make him become a priest." This statement contains astonishing distortions of the facts, as though the "kidnapping" had preceded the Baptism, as though it had been a violent act planned in order to turn the scion of a Jewish family into a Catholic priest. There is truly reason to worry if this is the version spread through the world even by diplomats of the State of Israel.

One look at the thousands of pages on the Internet is enough to make someone who knows how the events actually unfolded tear out his hair. The reports by Jewish and secular sources—and sometimes even by Catholics, at least those professing a certain type of Catholicism—is full of misunderstandings, ambiguities, and omissions. Above all, these pieces are marked by complete silence about Mortara's long life as a Christian.

The lad, as we know, soon disappointed those who sided with his defenders; he showed not only by words but also by deeds that he had found his true vocation; he testified to his boundless gratitude to the pope, whom they depicted as his executioner. Hence the polemicists dwelled always and exclusively on "the boy Edgardo", disregarding the adolescent, the young man, the adult, the old man, in short, first the novice and then Father Pio Maria, the impassioned preacher who never showed any hesitation, not only in thanking Pius IX but also in his fidelity to and love for the Church.

In the book by David I. Kertzer, only three pages out of more than three hundred are devoted to the man's later life. And yet this outcome is anything but irrelevant. Not only did the "victim" tenaciously insist on becoming a monk; he was by no means an ordinary religious, like so many. Gian Ludovico Masetti Zannini, a Church historian who has edited important, previously unpublished documents concerning the case, wrote:

> Even if he had not been the protagonist of the incident that goes by his name, Father Pio Mortara would rightly have a place in the history of the Order of Canons Regular, of which he is the glory because of the works that he was able to accomplish and because of his valuable pastoral activity.

Yet Kertzer is so little interested in the disappointing outcome of the incident in which the frightened "prisoner" sends away the "liberators", that to him the very long life that Edgardo spent in faithfulness to the gospel seems not to exist. His thick bibliography makes clear that this professor at the University of Providence, Rhode Island, consulted many archives, but not the most important one: the archive of the Canons Regular of the Lateran, which obviously contains a wealth of documentation about a religious who was an active, long-lived member. From the list of his sources it appears that Kertzer did not make it as far as the monastery of Saint Peter in Chains. And yet that is the location of the archive where, logically, I recovered the memoir that no one had taken the trouble to consult.

As the protagonist himself says in the pages that we are publishing: "Everyone, the great and the lowly, the famous and the unknown, the powerful and the insignificant, wanted to talk about the 'Mortara case'. Now at last let Mortara himself speak."

Kertzer notes:

> Specialists in Jewish studies anywhere in the world ... invariably knew ... the story of the little Jewish boy taken at the Inquisitor's order from his home. People who did not know the difference between Mazzini and Cavour knew everything about Edgardo and the illiterate Catholic servant who claimed to have baptized him.[3]

Did they really know "everything"? After so much talk by others, it is now—after almost a century and a half—the protagonist's turn to speak.

I already mentioned the fact that, in leafing through the memoir, anyone who is acquainted with the endless commentary, especially the journalism, written about the affair will realize that many things were either concealed or distorted.

One rather important thing, among others, is an authentic revelation that, I admit, I myself did not know about: namely, there was a recommendation by Pius IX himself that the child should not be brought to Rome but should be placed in an institute in Bologna, so that his parents could visit him easily whenever they liked. Only in response to the invincible resistance of the Mortaras, incited by various individuals, was the decision made to transport him to the capital.

It must be emphasized that, to a great extent, others caused the intransigent attitude of the family. *La Civiltà Cattolica* itself acknowledged this, noting how those

---

[3] Ibid., 300.

who had a political or ideological interest in not resolving the case in a less traumatic way used or even exploited the Mortaras. For those polemicists, indeed, the idea was to harden the positions so as to raise the stakes of the conflict. And this was so from the very beginning, from that refusal to allow the child to be sheltered in the same city.

It appears that Edgardo's father, Momolo, belonged to the Masonic lodge in Bologna. At the very least, he was a well-known sympathizer. In any event, Libero Muratore, the family physician, who was also a great friend of Momolo, certainly was a Freemason. Upon the arrival of the Piedmontese in Emilia, when the local inquisitor, a Dominican priest, was arrested and prosecuted (but swiftly acquitted of all charges, as we will see), the physician was the one who issued a polite certificate declaring that little Edgardo's illness many years before had not been serious at all and that, therefore, there was no cause for an emergency Baptism *in articulo mortis* (on the point of death). Yet all the testimonies, not only that of the maidservant who had administered the sacrament, speak about the parents' resigned desperation.

Certainly from him, from that doctor and from his fellows in the lodge, came the initial advice to be intransigent, to go head-to-head with the Church, which could not help but do what she deemed to be her strict and sacred duty yet was not at all ruthless, whatever the black legend may say, and was therefore quite amenable to all sorts of mitigation. In other words, she would preserve the principle of the thing while showing the greatest possible respect for the persons involved. Recall the words of the representative of the Roman Jews: "the benign and charitable nature of him who is seated on high".

After that local Mason intervened so promptly, all the others followed, one might say from all over the world.

The lodges took possession of the Mortara case (or rather, they themselves mightily helped to create it), considering it manna from Heaven: What better argument for their anti-Church propaganda? What more shameful act to pin on Pius IX, whose mortal remains a mob would one day try to throw into the Tiber, while Giuseppe Garibaldi, the grand master of the Sons of the Widow, described them with gentlemanly courtesy as "a cubic meter of manure"?

In general, all the politicians were *enchantés*: this was the term with which the Piedmontese ambassador in Turin described Napoleon III, who protected the Papal States with his troops so as to humor the French Catholics. The French emperor did not, in reality, support priests, pope, or Church, however, and he was likely a member of the Carbonari, which backed the movement to create a liberal and united Italy. The "flagrant return to the darkest Middle Ages", as he described the Mortara case, provided him with a valuable, unexpected argument for beginning to disengage himself from the protective role that earned him the reproaches of the anticlerical world.

More *enchanté* than anyone else was the Count of Cavour. It is no accident that, at the level of public opinion, the affair starts with the call to solidarity of all the Jews in the world, launched by the Piedmontese Jews gathered in Alessandria for one of their meetings. Cavour's private secretary was Isacco Artom, who being in close contact with his coreligionists in the other Italian states, quickly alerted him to what had happened in Bologna. The astute count, a political animal par excellence, immediately understood that he could take advantage of it. In fact, he played the card down the line and, we must admit, very profitably: the occupation of the Papal Legations in 1859, contrary to the treaty that had ended the second war of independence, was justified also by citing the Mortara case. It was necessary to put an end to a theocratic power as soon as possible, the Piedmontese said, if similar scandals were to be avoided.

For the Jews, too, the occasion was certainly not negligible: the abolition of the ghettos had been welcomed with relief, but nevertheless with some anxiety in more traditional Jewish circles. In fact, precisely that obligation to live all together, to make a common defense against the surrounding hostility, even at the cost of sufferings and humiliations, had preserved their identity and fostered their solidarity. As the Jewish historian Kertzer says, "Life in the ghetto had its joys and consolations."[4] Let us not forget that, from the times of the pre-Christian Diaspora, the Jewish population always sought to regroup in a separate district. The Muslims (the first to introduce the ghettos, even though the name is of Venetian origin) and then the Christians added—and it certainly was odious—a wall and gates that were closed and locked in the evening, but they did not invent the idea of Jewish concentration in an exclusive zone.

In the 1800s, with the new liberal laws, quite a few Jews looked anxiously at what was happening with the breakup of their common life: far from the ghetto, dispersed throughout the region, the Jews were assimilating; the number of mixed marriages increased; the old traditions were not respected as they once were; the orthodox religion was no longer easy to audit. Nevertheless, others complained, some Jews seemed not to realize the danger. The Mortara case demonstrated the need to remain united, to create solid organizations for self-defense, to rediscover the pride of being sons of Abraham

[4] Ibid., x.

and followers of the Mosaic Law. As I mentioned, it was no accident that the Alliance Israélite and the American Board were born of this situation, just as the occasion of the Dreyfus affair was taken to show that, however much they assimilated, the Jews were still in danger and therefore it was necessary for them to create a state where they would be masters in their own house.

In short, it must be said that from many sides (including the most influential, those capable of mobilizing and influencing public opinion) there was a decisive, deliberate exploitation that went so far as cynicism. The child and his fate mattered little or not at all to those whose consideration was the political, ideological, and confessional advantage that could be derived from the case. As previously mentioned, the secretary of the Roman Jews himself, Scazzocchio, felt "bitterness" and "anger" as a result and was convinced that in this way, instead of helping Edgardo, they were harming him.

That for at least some the attention was a means to an end, and the actual person was of no interest, is confirmed by what we have already noted: namely, that in order to keep the symbol and the myth alive, the real Mortara was erased, the one who found his home in the Church and was immediately, and forever, fervently grateful to Divine Providence for leading him to it.

The few references made—in the past or even today—to his life, first as an aspirant, then as a novice, and finally as a priest in the austere order that he had freely and willingly entered, have been to assert that this choice demonstrated even more clearly how monstrous Pius IX and his henchmen were. Those priests had succeeded in warping the mind of their prey, goes the argument, had convinced him of whatever they wanted, had turned him into a puppet, had infected him with what we call today Stockholm

syndrome: the morbid, pathological submission of a prisoner to his jailers. Yet with the passage of years it became
evident that the vocation of Edgardo, who became Pio
Maria, was quite solid, that it withstood every trial, that it
proved to be authentic. Thus, this chapter of his story has
been ignored. Listen to Kertzer:

> The child who had once been portrayed in the most glow-
> ing terms, the object of Jewish compassion, became a man
> who was disdained, whose character had to be discredited.
> He could not be happy, he could not even be fully sane,
> for were he happy and sane, it would reflect poorly on the
> religion of the Jews. It was best not to talk of him at all.[5]

According to the American historian, the disappointment
among many who fought for the boy to be returned to
his family was painful, because the conclusion of the incident showed that, when compared with what was
considered the most execrable sort of Catholicism, that
of the reactionary Pius IX, the Jews and the secularists
"lost the contest".

In his autobiography, Father Mortara bitterly mentions
this sometimes brutal exploitation of his person. Also
evident is his bitterness over the refusal, by all those
who said they wanted to help him, to believe in what
he unhesitatingly calls a miracle of grace. That is, he had
quickly noticed not only an attraction to Christianity but
also an immediate certainty that he had been impelled
toward the goal that he eagerly desired: the Church that
he did not know, but of which he had become a son,
albeit unwittingly until then.

[5] Ibid., 302.

Those who aimed at keeping alive the indignation over the kidnapping said that the priests were lying, that the poor child did nothing but weep and call for his parents, desiring nothing but to return to the religion of his birth. And then, when it was necessary to admit that Edgardo's spiritual well-being was real and not an invention by the clergy, there was talk about irresistible pressure, a plot against a minor, the diabolical cleverness of the Jesuits to destroy the will of a poor, defenseless individual.

After everyone has had his say, it is time to let the protagonist speak. For him (and here I paraphrase him) it is inexplicable, in human terms, how love and respect for his parents could coexist in his heart with the immediate and utmost determination not to return home, lest he risk losing the treasure of faith in Christ. For him there is no explaining his feelings, even during the journey that brought him to Rome, of attraction to churches, to the Mass, to prayers, to all Catholic realities. From the first moments, this attraction—again, in his words—dispelled his confusion, fear, and pain of separation, causing him to glimpse already the way to achieve his own destiny, even though he had been unaware of it until then. Mortara himself assures us of this, whereas Kertzer treats it ironically:

> Having been graced by divine light on his way to Rome, Edgardo, although only six, was blessed with a spiritual strength well beyond his years. Indeed, the story was so inspiring that it continued to be told for many decades— with significant variations in detail, though always with the same basic outline. In all versions of the story, Edgardo, on entering the Catechumens, eagerly sought to learn all he could about his new religion.[6]

[6] Ibid., 67.

The protagonist tells us that all this was true, regardless of historians who claim to reconstruct the events of a person's life while ignoring that person's own testimony. For this reason too, the American historian visited all the archives except the one belonging to the Canons Regular, which preserves a manuscript that speaks about a vocation that blossomed early and withstood all trials, so that the interested party himself does not hesitate to describe it as "miraculous".

As early as August 11, 1858, thus only a little more than a month and a half after the boy's separation from his family, the secretary of the Roman Jewish community, Sabatino Scazzocchio whom we have already met, wrote to the parents, in Bologna, that the first obstacle to face was, unpredictably, "the resistance manifested by Edgardo to returning to the practices of our religion". As a man of faith, Mortara would always view things from a faith perspective: Divine Providence, grace, vocation are for him not only words, but realities that displayed all their strength through the Baptism that grafted him onto the Body of Christ, the Church.

In a memoir written in 1908, fifty years after his entrance, at least his conscious entrance, into the ecclesial community, he said that he suddenly discovered that his soul was *naturaliter christiana* (naturally Christian). And he added:

> How else could I explain what I could call the explosion of Christian sentiment in my mind, immediately after receiving the first ideas about the faith? I did not know that there was a religion besides the one that my family professed. And yet, no sooner was I instructed in the rudiments of the catechism than I adhered to the Catholic Church and to her Head with a strength and a tenacity that nothing has been able to shake or conquer.

His nascent faith is an enigma that everyone ought to respect. This profound conviction of having been called, confirmed by a long life of apostolic labors, is a fact that must be faced honestly. For Christians, there is reason here to meditate on the mystery of Baptism and on its effects.

The point about Baptism is the decisive one that many involved in the case did not understand: whether because of true incomprehension of what was at stake or for the sake of exploitation, so as to derive confessional or political advantage from it.

We already said that the law and the practice of the Church forbade administering Baptism to Jewish children *invitis parentibus*, that is, without their parents' consent. It was permitted only in two cases: the abandonment of newborn children or the danger of death, when the medical arts ruled out the possibility of a return to life and health. In these two cases, and in them alone, Baptism was considered not only valid but also licit. In the case of little Edgardo, the sacrament was both valid and licit, given that the danger of death was imminent, whatever the physician may have said several years later.

Whenever any Christian, out of a deplorable zeal, had administered the sacrament apart from the two conditions, he was punished (as early as the beginning of the sixteenth century there was a fine for the enormous sum of two thousand scudi; for someone who could not pay, the equivalent in years at the oar of a papal galley) and the Baptism was considered illicit. The Church is firm on this point, because from the perspective of faith, the words, the intentions, and the sacramental water exert a mysterious but real force that infuses the grace won by Christ on the Cross and transforms the very nature of the baptized person. It is an indelible transformation. It is impossible to

reverse. For faith there is no option to "unbaptize". The
eyes of the "flesh" (to speak as Saint Paul does) do not dis-
cern this mystery, but the eyes of the spirit do.

Even today, most of the publicity would have us believe
that the Church had hastily taken possession of Edgardo,
without discernment, as though she desired to compel a
Jew to enter her sheepfold. The opposite is true: above all
in those very difficult times, with enemies watching her
every move, looking for any pretext to create a scandal
to accuse her of, both the pope and the whole hierarchy
would rather have done without a "case" like that.

Indeed, although the order to separate the child from his
family arrived toward the end of June 1858, in October
1857—we know from the documents—Father Pier Gaetano Feletti, inquisitor general in Bologna, already informed
the competent authorities in Rome that he had received
notice of a case of a Jewish boy baptized *in articulo mortis*
who unforeseeably had survived. The response from Rome
recommended investigating as discreetly as possible, but at
the same time in depth, whether the Baptism could be considered valid without any doubt. The investigations took
a good eight months. Only when there was certainty that a
new Christian had in fact entered the Church unexpectedly
did they proceed to contact the Mortaras to offer them the
conciliatory proposals that were discussed, only to proceed
ultimately by force, with the intervention of the police.

To those, even Catholics in good faith, who urged him
to return the child, Pius IX invariably replied: "*Non possumus.*" (We cannot.) Indeed, he truly could not; his faith
made him the prisoner of a mystery that is at the same time
extraordinary and awesome.

This is the perspective from which we must understand
some vivid and, to a nonbeliever, offensive expressions that

were used by Louis Veuillot, the editor-in-chief of *L'Univers*, the Catholic daily newspaper in Paris and mouthpiece of French Ultramontane Catholics, that is, a subset that was intensely faithful to the pope and therefore engaged in polemics against Gallicanism, Jansenism, and liberalism. Veuillot wrote: "The question is not whether to take a son from his natural father. Rather, it has to do with whether to prevent him from being snatched away from his new spiritual father." Pius IX made the same observation, bitterly and at the same time decisively: "The great and the insignificant tried to snatch this boy away from me, accusing me of being a ruthless barbarian. They commiserate with his parents and never think that I too am his father."

Some historians who are not friendly toward Pius IX recognize that he was a man with a delicate conscience, to the point of being liable to scruples. We have already mentioned Massimo d'Azeglio, who, pursuing a dual vocation as artist and politician, resided for a long time in the Papal States and on several occasions met Pius IX, against whom he then waged war as a statist. A Catholic liberal, d'Azeglio was harshly anticlerical and sharp in his judgments on the Vatican Curia. After one of his audiences with the pope, d'Azeglio described him in a private letter to Cesare Balbo:

> He has an extremely rare gift, the best of all in a leader, namely, a manifestation of such great sincerity in his look, in his face and in his words, that it is convincing and dispels the possibility of suspicion.

Much more of a pastor than a politician, much more candid than astute, this pontiff was incapable of falsehood. He was a priest who made painful, rigorous examinations of conscience, trusting in the mercy of Christ, whose vicar he was, and at the same time afraid of not living up to the gospel, knowing that he was supposed to be the greatest witness to it. Nevertheless, this sincere, scrupulous man, although beset by the storm that was raging halfway around the world, never had any hesitation, and years later he coolheadedly confirmed it on a public, solemn occasion: "What we did for that boy, We had the right and the duty to do. And if the opportunity presented itself, We would do it again."

The Church has proclaimed this pope Blessed, declaring his heroic virtues and proposing him therefore to the faithful as a role model and an intercessor. The tranquility of this pope's conscience says something, does it not, to Catholics at least?

Everyone in Bologna and Rome, however, was quite aware that he was experiencing a tragedy; no one minimized the suffering of the Mortara household. A significant comment was made by the commander of the papal gendarmerie in Bologna when he received the surely thankless assignment of taking the boy from his family to settle him in the carriage that was to take him to the capital: "Rather than that order, I would have preferred an order to arrest the most dangerous criminal of all."

To accompany Edgardo to Rome, they chose the father of a large family who knew what paternal feelings are. He was ordered not to wear his uniform so as not to frighten the boy, and he had strict orders to be as amiable as possible; they gave him sweets and toys for the boy. To many people—how to put it?—such "palliative" measures may seem not a sign of humanity but of even more refined barbarity, like the hypocrisy of the executioner, the last meal, the last cigarette for the condemned man. I realize this. But precisely in order to avoid the possibility of this type of suffering, the Church had issued the law forbidding non-Christians to hire Christian domestic help, which the family in Bologna had violated. The Mortaras knew the rules yet acted against them; the whole thing started with their transgression.

Let us not forget: Pius IX was not only head of the Church but also the temporal head of the Papal States. He was therefore, still, a pope-king—a disputed position, against which many enemies were militating and which twelve years later was to end (providentially, as Paul VI acknowledged in 1970, with the distance of a century of history). The fact remains that in 1858, not only canon law but also civil law required that someone baptized validly—regardless of the conditions in which the sacrament had been administered—should be raised as a Christian. The code of the Papal States was quite clear about this, and let us not forget that this was the oldest state in Europe, recognized by all the powers that maintained regular diplomatic relations with it. Incumbent upon Pius IX, therefore, was not only a religious but also a political duty, in the sense that it was necessary for him to uphold respect for the laws of which he was the source, the guarantor, and the guardian. Whether or not they were agreeable is not the point; in any case, they were in force, and it was necessary to comply with them.

Louis Veuillot, as usual, used no politically correct euphemisms, but his objectivity cannot be denied, although it is a bit brutal:

> The Mortaras, like the many other Jews who for centuries have lived in the papal lands, knew very well the laws that were in force there. If they were not agreeable to them, they could have moved elsewhere, even just to neighboring Piedmont, where, with the statute, other laws had been in force for a decade. Well then: the Mortaras broke those laws *first*, by hiring Anna Morisi; *afterward* they

claimed that the Head of those domains himself was the one to break them by not enforcing a precise rule.

Furthermore *La Civiltà Cattolica*, too, recalled that the Mortaras

transgressed the ordinances enacted to ensure their rights, ordinances designed so that the ill-advised zeal of one of those servants would not impel him to do something that could be repaired only by a rather bitter severance.

The Jesuit biweekly added considerations about the law that was the basis for the decision to take Edgardo from his family:

Were the Mortaras perhaps unaware that this and no other legislation was in force in the Papal State? Were the many Jews who lived in their household unaware too? When they, therefore, settled in Bologna, they were subject to all the laws that are in force there and they were reckoned to have accepted them tacitly. Of course, if those laws had seemed too difficult for them, they were completely free to go elsewhere. But if they and their fellow believers want to remain there, it is bad manners to expect that canon and state law be modified to suit them.

The Jesuits of that era, as we know, were rather forthright and did not mince words, so much so that once before they had provoked so many strong reactions that the pope at the time had been compelled to suppress the Society so as to escape the wrath of the powerful.

Still, anyone truly acquainted with the incident knows that nothing was done frivolously. The authorities in Rome were well aware that two rights were in conflict: the natural right of parents to educate their children and the right of the baptized child to experience the spiritual riches of Baptism and to be safeguarded from dangers to his faith in the case of a return to his family. Nevertheless, the Catholic perspective is based on a hierarchy that cannot possibly be ignored without unhinging the doctrine of the faith itself: when a right in the natural order conflicts with another in the supernatural order, the latter necessarily prevails.

It is significant that at least some of the Jews who protested as religious persons realized that the pope was motivated by no interest other than the religious one, and they understood the logic of faith that guided the Church. Therefore, instead of ridiculing the "irrevocable" character of Baptism as though it were medieval obscurantism, instead of mocking the Catholic conviction that the sacrament is effective *ex opere operato*, as so many secular individuals did, there were efforts to obtain the return of Edgardo by seeking to prove either that the story was an invention of the maidservant and no Baptism had been administered or that the canonical norms had not been observed and, therefore, the Baptism could be declared invalid.

But, as was mentioned, many months of investigation proved that Edgardo had in fact become a Christian and therefore had to be entrusted to the Church onto which he had been grafted—at least (and this must not be forgotten!) until he reached the age of majority, when, if he had wanted to, no one could have prevented him from returning to the religion of his fathers. Giacomo Cardinal Antonelli, Pius IX's secretary of state, personally assured the boy's father, Momolo, that the time of the lad's free choice would come "when he turned seventeen".

Hence one of Louis Veuillot's paradoxes, which were so irritating and scandalous that Daniele Scalise, the author of a recent book on the case, indulges in the not always well-informed indignation that inspires his pages: "Every century has a pantheon of depraved individuals. In the nineteenth century a place of honor surely belongs to Louis Veuillot."

Matters are often much more complex than those who engage in polemics are willing to admit. Thus, they raise their voices, inveighing against the "depravity" of a man, a convert, whose ideas and style divided Catholics themselves and who understood his role as an intellectual in military terms. Yet he was the first journalist—and, as far as I know, the only one—to whom a pope who was later beatified ever sent a letter of gratitude and solidarity while being persecuted by the tyrannical power of an emperor.

To illustrate the fascination with and the impact of Veuillot's vibrant and at the same time dry prose, interwoven with facts that had the enemies of the Church with their backs to the wall: The French government had despoiled the clergy of all their temporal goods, including the properties of parish churches, and did not even provide a stipend for parish priests. The latter, often extremely poor, lived in the countryside, supported by the charity of farmers, and could not afford a subscription to *L'Univers*. So as not to miss a daily reading that they thought invaluable, many of those priests contributed a fraction of the cost and organized as follows: the first one to receive the newspaper early in the morning read it quickly and fastened the copy to the collar of a dog that was trained to run to the neighboring rectory. The second priest read it and then entrusted to another dog the delivery of the daily paper to a third confrere. And so it went until evening, when all the priests of the region had been able to read Veuillot's editorial, from which they often took a cue for their homilies.

Veuillot was a journalist for whom, as is plain from the pages of the memoir, Mortara himself would express his gratitude and esteem. Scalise imagines that he is defending the "kidnapped boy" by insulting Veuillot; but that "kidnapped boy" praised Veuillot to the skies. Such odd contradictions run all through this case.

However, here is Veuillot, whose irony was the scourge of those who were attacking the Church:

> You protest, but are you not the same ones who claim freedom of conscience at all costs? Tell me, then: might young Mortara not be the one who is in the best position to choose his religion freely, according to his knowledge and conscience? The rabbis would not have taught him the Law of Christ. The priests cannot raise him without teaching him the Law of Moses. Now he is still young but, once he has reached the age of majority, in a world like the present one, in which no human ordinance punishes apostasy, he will be able to decide freely for himself between the two Laws.

It must be noted that Veuillot is not being doctrinaire and inhumane or ignoring the boy's feelings: he had become acquainted with him in Rome and had had the opportunity to speak with him at length, discovering that his Christian vocation and gratitude toward the pope had been manifested quite vividly.

Given his fondness for paradox, however, the militant publicist found something providential in the explosion of the affair:

> It does, of course, present some inconvenience of a temporal sort; it poses diplomatic and political problems for the Holy See. But to me the advantage in the spiritual order seems great: indeed, it reminds Catholics, who

have trivialized the truths of the faith, how important
Baptism is. Pius IX is willing to lose all that remains of
his States, but not to allow one soul to be lost, even that
of a humble boy.

As we will see, in the text translated here, Father Mortara dwells for a long time precisely on the value of Baptism from the perspective of Saint Thomas Aquinas,
Doctor of the Church. Not by chance, this is the most
theological part of the autobiography. Although these lines
may seem complex or even arid, in reality they are per-
vaded by the passion of a staunch faith that reflects on its
reasons for believing.

It is striking, and even saddening, that the religious dimen-
sion that was understood by at least some Jews in the nineteenth century seems foreign to some Catholics today. I
alluded earlier to the polemics provoked by the publica-
tion, in the largest Italian daily newspaper, of an alleged
1945 document of the Holy See that set for the Church in
France rules of conduct for the return of Jewish children
who had been sheltered in convents so that they might
escape the Nazis. The historian who had published that
document replied to numerous serious challenges with
another article, in which, instead of defending himself,
he decided to attack. That scholar calls himself a practicing Catholic and is considered one. For this reason, too, I
reacted, and after a piece in that same daily newspaper
I published another in a weekly. Allow me, for conve-
nience' sake, to reprint a passage on the specific topic that
interests us here:

> In his disconcerting reply, the historian-journalist dismisses
> the problems posed for faith by Baptism administered

to children by describing the prudent measures recommended by the Church as "ordinances of a frozen theological bureaucracy". This is astonishing. Therefore, all the extremely rich reflection over the centuries about the mystical value of the primordial sacrament, the one that engrafts souls onto the Church, is described as nothing but "theological bureaucracy".

Here, indeed, one of the exclamation points that the journalist used in his articles would be appropriate, given that a similar scornful, vexed dismissal of the effects of Baptism is made by someone who calls himself Catholic.

I continued:

Precisely because he was aware of the mysterious but real consequences of Baptism, Blessed Pius IX confronted the violent storm of the one that became "the Mortara case". Along the same lines that had been established over the centuries, the Church, after the disaster and the chaos of World War II, was concerned and set precise rules whenever some Jewish child entrusted to her care had been baptized. If this had happened, the irresponsible person who baptized would have gone against every canonical norm, against all tradition, which always condemned (except in a few extreme cases) administering Baptism to children whose parents were unaware of it or opposed to it. But what was to be done if, unfortunately, it had occurred? Was it not the responsibility of the Church, who is a Mother, to inquire about the fate of that child who was unexpected but is now entrusted to her? Are such precautions, concerns, regulations really nothing but "frozen theological bureaucracy"? It is not encouraging to have to ask such questions. And it is astonishing that a brand of Catholicism that looks forward to a Vatican III should come to this, after dismissing the most elementary truths of the catechism with the disdain of someone who is above such "bureaucracies".

In any case, those Catholics who blame Pius IX for his tenacity—and Pius XII for his prudence—often do not know that they are setting themselves, once more today, against the fundamental law of the Church. Indeed, here is canon 868, paragraph 2, of the new *Code of Canon Law*, promulgated in 1983 and composed entirely according to the letter and the spirit of Vatican Council II: "An infant of Catholic parents or even of non-Catholic parents is baptized licitly in danger of death even against the will of the parents." Canon 794 of the same *Code* recalls in paragraph 1: "The duty and right of educating belongs in a special way to the Church, to which has been divinely entrusted the mission of assisting persons so that they are able to reach the fullness of the Christian life." And the second paragraph of the same canon adds: "Pastors of souls have the duty of arranging everything so that all the faithful have a Catholic education."[7]

Therefore, despite the thoughtless announcements of contemporary experts in politically and ecumenically correct speech, who are ready to free themselves from everything that is not in line with the conformism of modern right thinking, the postconciliar Church has not denied (nor could she have done so) the theological foundations that dictated the attitude of Pius IX. As one scandalized journalist wrote on one of the many aggressive websites, after learning about the *Code of Canon Law*: "Therefore the impossibility of a new Mortara case is to be ascribed to the changed balance of power between the Church and society and by the disappearance of a temporal State led by the Pope, not to the abjuration of the juridical norms that made it possible."

[7] *Code of Canon Law*, English translation prepared under the auspices of the Canon Law Society of America (Rome: Libreria Editrice Vaticana, 1983), http://www.vatican.va/archive/ENG1104/_INDEX.HTM.

The fact remains that underlying these juridical norms is a baptismal theology, Sacred Scripture with its requirements, and a faith perspective confirmed by twenty centuries of Tradition, which the Church cannot deny without denying herself.

As I said, I stand with Paul VI. Therefore, for what my opinion is worth, I too consider the purpose of papal governance providential. In a conversation with Hermann Kanzler, the commander of his troops, shortly before the invaders began to fire on the Porta Pia, Pius IX uttered the following remark: "The temporal authority is a sacred thing, I will defend it to the death, but it is a big nuisance." A nuisance, certainly, but necessary today as well, even though adapted to the times.

Indeed, the resistance of Pope Pius IX and of his successors—their decision to enclose themselves in the Vatican, declaring themselves prisoners and victims of an outrage—was providential. Only this intransigence allowed them to salvage the essential principle that, in order to be free in her spiritual activity, the Church must be free from external political impositions. Therefore, she must be mistress in her own house; she must not be the guest of some earthly grandee, as were the patriarch of Constantinople and the popes in Avignon, who quickly became courtiers and then puppets manipulated by the Byzantine emperor and the king of France, respectively.

Pius IX was clear-sighted and rejected traps such as the Law of Guarantees, proposed by the king of Italy. It was a seemingly generous law, but in reality it declared the state the sole owner, which, as long as it served its own interest, benevolently and royally granted hospitality on lands that it had seized in cold blood, without even the pretext of a declared war. If it were not for Pope Pius IX and the pontiffs who succeeded him until 1929, they would never have arrived at the Lateran Treaty with its suitable formula for the Vatican City State, which is the smallest state in the world (a little more than 100 acres), with a population, an army, and an administrative structure that are little more than symbolic, but is nevertheless a sovereign state, on a par with any other, in which the pope is also the king, with all that this political independence signifies for his spiritual independence, the only kind that matters. Benedetto Croce described the Law of Guarantees as "a monument of legal wisdom", but he, a secularist, approved of it precisely from the perspective of the state's exclusive interest. He nevertheless acknowledged that the Church "needs a minimal amount of body in order to bind your souls".

Even though the Vatican is once again a state, a Mortara case, though possible in theory, will no longer be possible in practice. No papal gendarmerie today will take a child away from his family in order to give him a Catholic education until he reaches majority. I am the first to rejoice that tragedies like this, which confront parents with heart-rending alternatives, are unthinkable. But at the same time it should be noted that even the postconciliar Church has not denied but has confirmed the theological principles from which Pius IX inferred consequences that enraged so many enemies against him. There is in the faith a strict logic, in which each truth presupposes another and leads to still another. We cannot and should not be nostalgic for the type of temporal power that Pius IX defended, being unable to do otherwise; but Catholics ought to want the principles to be safeguarded. And this is what the *Code of Canon Law* does, it has been noted, in a Church that is engaged in interfaith dialogue but does not therefore forget the requirements of what the Germans call, or used to call (even dedicating university professorships to it), *die katholische Weltanschauung* (the Catholic worldview).

One of the things missing from the endless columns that have dealt with Mortara is mention of the fact that one country was absent from the uprising of European politicians and diplomats against Pius IX—and not an insignificant one. There was no protest from the largest, together with France, of the continental empires; or, at least, if at first there were a few voices, they quickly fell silent. Austria-Hungary, indeed, had a law stating that anyone who baptized a Jewish child against his parents' wishes was sentenced to two years in prison and a fine of a thousand gold coins. If it turned out, however, that this illicit Baptism had been administered validly, Austrian law (although marked by the eighteenth-century secularism of Joseph II) prescribed that the child be "separated from the parents at once and raised as a Christian by honest persons", at the expense of the "wild" baptizer. If the latter had no means of paying, the child had to be placed in a state institution "until he had learned a profession". After that, he was free to choose what direction to give to his life.

Vienna in the second half of the nineteenth century was not a place of obscurantist barbarians and fanatical rubes, but one of the most brilliant, most admired capitals of the "enlightened" world—a place where life was pleasant and extremely civil, so much so that nostalgia for it persists even today. The parliamentary empire with Vienna at its heart was certainly more democratic than the authoritarian France of Napoleon III or than England itself, where power was concentrated in the hands of a small aristocratic caste and only a miniscule percentage of the population could run for office. Nevertheless, the Austrian law duplicated that of the Papal States, and no one was scandalized by it.

No insults or threats came from Vienna, therefore, but rather the acknowledgment that the pope had acted just as the imperial government would have conducted itself in similar circumstances. This is not an incidental matter, because it shows that Rome was really not isolated or alone in following principles and practices from centuries past.

Therefore, we find consistency on the part of the Church, whether yesterday or—despite everything—today. And it is not surprising, obviously, that we are talking about a consistency that causes indignation in those who do not understand or do not accept the theoretical and practical consequences of the faith. That is part of the logic of things, the logic of "not being conformed to the world", a scriptural expression that always means accepting the gospel perspective.

It must be added, nevertheless, that there is incoherence and even hypocrisy on the part of the so-called secularists, especially the politicians. We see, then, that we are broadening our outlook to general considerations, starting from this particular case, which at the same time is exemplary.

Let us speak, therefore, about Camillo di Cavour, who, they used to say, did all he could to inflate the affair; he, indeed, was among the master craftsmen who created it. It was no accident that, with lightning speed, he took advantage of the meeting of Piedmontese Jews in Alessandria to make an appeal to all Europe. When the Mortara case took on dimensions that were at first continental and then worldwide, the synergy between him, his government, and international Judaism became ever closer.

Indeed, the king of Sardinia was living thanks to loans from Baron James Rothschild, the leader of Jewish finance who influenced the economy of many states in Europe. This included the Papal States, which drew vital oxygen, obviously at high interest rates, for its not very flourishing economy from the legendary banking family, which had branches in the major capitals. The pope too, therefore, was in the book of the Rothschilds' debtors.

But let us stay with Piedmont. After the Battle of Novara, the defeat that in 1849 ended the war with Austria, the peace treaty imposed on it an enormous indemnity of two hundred million lire. Since paying a sum like that meant bankruptcy for the king of Sardinia, which would have damaged his reputation, the Rothschilds, who had long been the chief creditors of Turin, intervened with Austria and succeeded in reducing the sum to seventy-five million. Baron James, therefore, could boast of momentous rights with regard to the Piedmontese, who, with Cavour and his policy of rearmament and infrastructures, especially railroads, became even more indebted to him. At the time of Italian unification, Sardinia would be the Italian state with the most financial troubles, with accounts that were totally out of control. The despised king of the Two Sicilies had balanced the books and some years even showed a surplus; the administration of Lombardo-Venice, which appears to have cost Austria more than it paid back, was nevertheless a model of accounts in order; although modest in scale, the Duchies of Parma and Modena and the Grand Duchy of Toscana (Tuscany) were doing tolerably well also. The Piedmontese policy of confiscating Church goods contravened the statute itself: "All properties, with no exception whatsoever, are inviolable." There was much boasting about the statute, but it had force only when it did not conflict with the liberals' policy. The statute was violated by considering "inviolable" all properties—starting, obviously, with the extensive holdings of the Cavours and of the other notables in the government—except those of the Church. This exception was certainly due to an anticlerical mind-set, out of hatred for "the priests", but it was also out of desperation, in order to scrounge up money with which to make payments to the bankers on their loans at the proper interest rates.

The tie between the king of Sardinia and the immense capital of the Rothschilds became so close as to cause Cavour to utter, in a private letter, expressions of intolerance: "Foreign Jews are the masters of our finances. That baron is strangling us." As a matter of fact, James Rothschild—together with other powerful Jews, such as Sir Moses Montefiore, the first Jew named baronet by the Crown of England, to whom was assigned the task of protector of Israel—took the Mortara incident very much to heart and contributed to the international mobilization of his coreligionists. Several times he spoke about it to Cardinal Antonelli, the Vatican secretary of state, insinuating that Pius IX's refusal to send the boy home could have repercussions on the flow of money that propped up the Papal States. Because the pope's determination, however, was unshakable—based as it was on the awareness that he was doing what he could not fail to do—he did not hesitate when faced with either political or economic pressure.

To return to Cavour, in the collection of his letters there are many exchanges with the Alliance Israélite Universelle, which had just been founded. In a confidential letter written in French and dated October 3, 1860—thus more than two years after the case burst onto the scene—the Piedmontese statesman continued to reassure the Jewish world:

The King's government will do everything in his power to make sure that that child, in whom public opinion in Europe has taken such a lively interest, is returned to his family.

Among other things, the mention of top-ranking figures in the world economy calls to mind that it is necessary to discredit the assertion that, when their son was taken away, the Mortaras suffered economic ruin because the sudden shock and the need to travel here and there to regain the child ruined their business of haberdashery, lace trimming, and used clothing and reduced them to pitiful poverty.

Pio Edgardo refers to this claim in his autobiography; he mentions it in order to deny it. Here are his rather drastic words:

> This sequestration [of the son] was the beginning, if not precisely of an enrichment, then at least of a well-being that they had not enjoyed before. Indeed, generous donations were sent to Signor and Signora Mortara by those who pretended hypocritically to lament their lot and their misfortune. The name Mortara acquired unexpected celebrity. In the commerce, in the industry, and in the other activities to which the Mortara brothers devoted themselves, this name was a sort of very prestigious label that could not help attracting remarkable material advantages.

Indeed, we know from many sources that, despite the legend claiming that the Mortaras were reduced to poverty, the contrary is true: the family was showered with economic assistance from the whole Jewish world, and not just from the millionaires such as those whom we have mentioned. Jewish communities in France and England, and the Italian communities themselves, made lucrative arrangements so that the father of the kidnapped boy could

travel around Europe to keep alive the news of the incident and to stir up indignation against the Church.

From Bologna the family moved to Turin, not acci-
dentally, and received a fine welcome from a government
that was friendly. Next they moved to Florence. That was
where Momolo Mortara would be tried for homicide (and
acquitted), after being accused of having thrown one of
his maidservants out of a window.[8] What an odd fate: one
maidservant had turned his life upside down when he was
young; another maidservant turned it upside down again
in his old age.

As proof that the family was well-to-do, Mortara's
many sons were able to study, and some took degrees.
One became an officer in the Italian army, and all had
good or at least decent careers and ended up establishing
normal relations with their brother, who had become a
famous Catholic missionary. When possible, they used to
meet (there are photos that depict them together) in fraternal serenity.

Indeed, Edgardo's refusal to go back home, given the
danger to his choice of Christianity that he perceived
there, never meant any lessening of his love for his family,
which was always very fervent. Precisely because he loved
them, he was consumed, as he used to say, with the desire that "the blindfold might fall from their eyes" and that
they might finally recognize that the Messiah whom they

---

[8] In April 1871 one of the Mortaras' maids, Rosa Tognazzi, was found dying
in the courtyard after falling from a balcony of the house. It seemed to be a sui-
cide, but further police investigation concluded that the girl had been severely
injured in the head during an altercation with Momolo, Edgardo's father. To
hide the violence, and with the help of a friend who was present on the prem-
ises, the man allegedly threw Rosa from the balcony. Mortara was imprisoned,
and his case was sent to the Court of Appeals, which on October 27 acquitted
him. When released he was already very ill, and he died shortly after.

were awaiting had arrived in the Nazarene whose apostle he had become.

Cavour—to return to him—was therefore interested in the Mortara case also by way of the Jewish world. But, of course, this was a stimulus that he would not have needed, so obvious was the political advantage of that child "kidnapped" by a despised pope, a pope who had already had serious conflicts with the Kingdom of Sardinia because of its policy of aggressive anticlericalism and whose dominions were the object of Turin's expansionist greed. Many historians are convinced of it: without this incident in Bologna, the count would have had difficulty in convincing Napoleon III to intervene, exactly one year later, against Austria and on the side of Piedmont.

The French Catholics did not want this war. These were the same Catholics who, embarrassed by the Mortara case and by the obsessive propaganda that the liberal press had patched together about him, raised only a weak protest when, violating armistices and treaties, the Piedmontese took possession of the Papal Legations by the technique of fait accompli. The occupation came about after the Piedmontese paid, through their agents, for supposedly "popular revolts" that called for them to reestablish order, and after the farce of the fraudulent referendum that caused embarrassment or hilarity throughout Europe.

As proof of the solidarity of the Church, which reflected at that time the mood of most of the common people, it must also be recalled that throughout the Diocese of Bologna not a single priest could be found willing to sing the Te Deum in San Petronio, as demanded by the subalpine forces that persecuted clergy, confiscated convents, and invaded papal lands, but pretended nevertheless to thank God for their "victories", which were obtained, incidentally, without their having fired a single shot. For a long time in Bologna, the liturgies desired by the new arrivals had to be celebrated by the military chaplains of the army of the king of Sardinia.

Piedmontese rage exploded at last when Vittorio Emanuele II came to visit the city that had been annexed. Once again there was general refusal by the clergy, not only to participate in the religious ceremonies but also to sound the bells as a sign of "festivity". Unable to arrest the archbishop, the severe, highly respected Michele Cardinal Viale-Prelà, because he was on his deathbed during those days, the Piedmontese arrested the vicar-general and sentenced him to three years of imprisonment and an enormous fine for having said that the bells would not be rung in the diocese, given that there was nothing to celebrate.

In their liberalism those gentlemen did not like to release on bail anyone who did not conform. It certainly was not liberal either to arrest in the middle of the night the old Dominican priest Pier Gaetano Feletti, with a great display of public force that was altogether illegal because it had no judicial authorization whatsoever. That priest, who was responsible for the tribunal of the Inquisition in Bologna, was indicted on the basis of a legal monstrosity: in effect, having been an official of the papal government (what remained of the Inquisition was a public office), he was summoned to answer for having observed the law in force in his state and for having obeyed the orders of his government and, therefore, for having arranged the separation of the child from his family. It was a monstrosity, it was said, according to which all officials of all defeated states would have to be put on trial for having observed the laws of their legitimate government before the defeat and the invasion. Father Feletti was imprisoned and had to do several months of hard time, and when he was tried, with great embarrassment (this was the first trial of the Piedmontese administration), he was swiftly acquitted on the same day and immediately released for the reason that ought to have been obvious from the start: "The removal of young Mortara was an act of the Prince and therefore there is no reason for criminal proceedings against those who carried out the aforesaid removal."

As David I. Kertzer notes, this trial appeared so embarrassing to everyone that no one protested against the acquittal, not even the most excited of those who had called for the arrest and the trial of the old Dominican. He finally was able to depart unhindered for Rome. When he arrived, Pius IX praised the resolute dignity with which he had faced the events: he had refused a defense attorney, not wishing to lend legitimacy to an illegal trial, and he had not answered those who interrogated him, recalling that he was bound by the secrecy of his office. Also in Rome he had the joy of being feted, embraced, and warmly thanked by, of all people, the very young Mortara, whose jailer he had been accused of being. As long as he lived, the "merciless inquisitor" was surrounded by the deferential gratitude of his "victim", who considered him a sort of beneficent, venerable uncle.

And let us mention only once—so as not to become too long-winded, while still providing a description of the milieu of the founding fathers of unified Italy—the fact that in addition to the illegal trial against the father inquisitor there was the grotesque case of Filippo Curletti.

He was a trusted agent of Cavour, who personally decided to send him from Turin to the invaded territories of Romagna as director general of police. Curletti, rigid and zealous to the point of ruthlessness, was the one who took the Dominican's case in hand, organized his spectacular arrest, pressured all possible witnesses, and incited the magistrates to make an example of the accused. With the new constitutional government, Curletti argued, there must be an end to the Church's corruption, superstition, and inequality. Even on the unhappy lands of the priests, he proclaimed, the sun of the new age had arisen, and figures like that fat friar, that vile Feletti, had to be rendered incapable of doing any more harm and had to atone for his crimes.

Kertzer cannot avoid mentioning the fate of Feletti, relegating these words to a footnote:

> A year later, Curletti would himself end up in a Turin jail, awaiting trial for murder in a complex tangle involving charges of organizing gangs of thieves and committing political assassinations. In the face of his threats that he would tell all about the secret misdeeds of Farini, Cavour, and other architects of the new state, his wardens allowed him to escape.[9]

After he fled, Curletti continued his blackmail and, in fact, published a dossier with many truths that were embarrassing for the Piedmontese government. At that point, Cavour and his men became so threatening that, to keep from being killed, Curletti emigrated to America. He was hunted down even there by hired assassins of the *Italianissimi* (extreme Italians), as Catholics called the patriots who sought unity at all costs.

However, to continue with the hypocrisies, this Cavour, who became indignant about the "barbarities of the papal kidnapping", only a few years before, without anyone

[9] Ibid., 321n4.

having asked him to, had allied himself with France and England to help Turkey against Russia.

Secular, civil Europe, therefore, helped Turks who for many centuries had an elite military force, the Janissaries, that was based on a criminal form of recruitment. The sultan had the finest, strongest male children snatched from the Christian families in his European possessions. The boys were raised according to the strictest form of Islam and then incorporated into an exclusive militia that was preferably deployed against Christian adversaries. The custom must have been very amusing to the Muslim political and religious leaders.

Among the regular practices of the Turks was another kind of forced abduction of sons of Christians: these boys were castrated by the removal or the crushing of their testicles. The Ottoman emperor needed eunuchs, not only to deploy in the harems of the sultan and of other rich dignitaries, but also because a castrated man, having neither children nor family, in a society afflicted by nepotism and corruption, was considered more trustworthy for public duties, more immune to temptations. In this case, however, the policy was to seize baptized boys and raise them like the Janissaries, as the most doctrinaire Islamists. As late as 1878, at the Congress of Berlin, the European powers, starting with Great Britain, mobilized to save the regime that instituted these practices from the dissolution that threatened it.

Every year, therefore, there were thousands of cases among the Turks that were infinitely crueler than the Mortara case. Yet to help the Turks, Cavour—shoulder to shoulder with France and England, which also mobilized their diplomatic forces and their press against Pius IX—sent fifteen thousand Piedmontese, who, practically speaking, had never been deployed in battle (the Battle of

Chernaya was nothing but an irrelevant skirmish) and died en masse from cholera, starting with their commander, Alessandro La Marmora.

The soldiers in the Crimean War as well as those, in 1859, in the new war desired by Cavour himself and by Napoleon III were conscripts, obliged to join the army by the universal draft, to which every family had to pay its tribute. The Catholics themselves forgot (amnesia seems to be their problem) their long, albeit useless, opposition to this horrible practice, commanded for the first time by the French Revolution and totally unknown during the Christian Middle Ages and the ancien régime. The Church, in her realism, did not fritter her time away with utopias of perpetual, universal peace, knowing that only the end of history will be able to bring it about. Therefore, as long as she could, she sought to restrict war, to limit it, to confine it to the confrontation of troops of volunteers, mercenaries who aimed to do themselves as little harm as possible. As long as she was obeyed by the peoples, she imposed increasingly strict rules: "God's truces", which permitted combat only on certain days, required the liberation of prisoners at Easter, and banned the provisioning troops at the expense of the population. Above all, to safeguard the youth, the Church taught that military service should be reserved to professionals who enlisted voluntarily. The French Revolution, in contrast, wanted war to be "of the people" and therefore to be "total", involving everyone.

Hence *la levée en masse* (mass conscription), which had been initiated by the Jacobin republic, was diabolically perfected by Napoleon (almost three million dead for his glory; the few months of his Russian campaign destroyed many more young lives than three centuries of Crusades). The draft then became the common practice of all the

European states, with the exception of England, which made it a point of honor not to follow the revolutionary innovations—for as long as it could, that is, because in the two world wars it drafted men from the ages of sixteen to sixty.

Thus, beginning in the nineteenth century, in peacetime or in war, a distant, unknown government, in a far-off European capital, demanded that the male children, in the flower of youth, right when they could help their families, be handed over. For at least three years (the average duration of compulsory enlistment) the state would do what it wanted with those young men and often would send them to die, maybe even from cholera in Crimea, where, as everyone knows, the king of Sardinia had major vital interests. If they managed to return home, they would have been trained to accept views contrary to the Catholic faith and morals of their parents.

Could a political class or a society become indignant about the Mortara case when it was not scandalized by the conscription of young men—to make them cannon fodder at the behest of their governments and, in any event, to raise them not to worship God but to worship the modern deities of nation, fatherland, and state—but instead regarded it as a source of nationalistic satisfaction? *La Civiltà Cattolica* denounced this in one of its articles on the case, recalling "the compulsory conscription that truly snatches youths from their homes and from the affection of their dear parents, not to place them in a boarding school, but to send them to confront either the spears of the Bedouins in the sunburned deserts of Africa or the Russian artillery on the unhealthy shores of inhospitable Tauris [Crimea]".

The Third French Republic, the political expression of Freemasonry, invested all the money and energies that it had available, after financing the army for *la revanche* (its revenge) against the Prussians, on the creation of a "compulsory school" that would make every little French boy a *citoyen*. That itself was not a neutral term, because by "citizen" they meant only someone who had been raised to revere the "immortal principles" of the Revolution. For those rabid anticlericals, elementary school was a sort of new secular seminary, entrusted to a corps of *instituteurs*, suitably trained instructors, so that in every village in France there would be an anticlerical alternative to the *curé*, the pastor.

All the countries in Europe adapted to the French model, including Italy, which, with the law introduced by Michele Coppino, expelled from schools all references to religion and replaced religion with "civic education" based on the Masonic "virtues". The children's book *Cuore* (Heart) by Edmondo De Amicis, with its missionary secular schoolmasters, is the literary illustration of the principles on which this teaching was based. School attendance, even in Italy, was mandatory; the carabinieri showed up at the houses of noncompliant parents. Education, therefore, was snatched away from parents: Catholics saw their sons led, if necessary *manu militari* (by armed force), to classrooms where the faith was mocked or, in the best possible case, disdainfully ignored as a meaningless or even harmful superstition.

How many "Mortara cases" were there, then, in thousands of families of believers? And their collective sequestration was not condemned as a sign of violence and expropriation of parental authority but, on the contrary, was exalted as the expression of civil progress, while ruinous laws closed the Catholic institutes so as not to give the parents alternatives! A deafening shout arose against a Church that claimed one child. Meanwhile there was

general consent to the terrible maxim that children belonged not to their parents but, first and foremost, to the
state: first with the school that trained them in an irre-
ligious outlook, and then with the military draft, which
often, at the whim of the political class of the moment, led
them to their death.

While we are on the subject of hypocrisy: as Pius IX
himself bitterly remarked (there are traces of bitterness in
Mortara's autobiography too), while the whole world was
indignant about the little boy from Bologna, the czar
was proceeding to commit one of the most monstrous acts
of cultural genocide—which met with total silence from
the European powers. In an attempt to have done with
Poland's irredentism, the Russians sequestered the sons
of the leading Catholic families so as to deport them and
raise them in boarding schools run by the Orthodox clergy.

The human "spoils" desired by the czar, as the supreme
representative of the national church, had grown even
more as a result of the Russian law decreeing that in the
case of a mixed marriage between Catholic and Orthodox parties, the sons had to be baptized by the Orthodox
priests and raised in their faith, even if both parents were
against it. Father Giacomo Martina, the Jesuit historian and
greatest biographer of Pius IX writes: "No liberal in Italy
or in other nations of Europe was ever concerned about
the severe limits set on religious freedom in the territories
subject to the czar."

The opinions of Polish fathers and mothers were not
among the things to be taken into consideration by the
opinion makers of nineteenth-century Europe. Therefore,
not only was there no protest by the people who were
indignant about the Mortara child, but there was even
hostility toward Poland's cause, because as Pierre-Joseph

Proudhon, the first political theorist to call himself an anarchist, spells out: "If Poland became independent we would find another Catholic nation underfoot, whereas our duty is to destroy the ones that are already there."

As often is the case—and in the case that interests us here—politics and ideology are selective with their emotions and indignation. Some might prefer to speak about hypocrisy, that is, the human trait that arouses the greatest indignation in the Gospels.

Something similar was happening in Great Britain. That country, involved all over the world in colonial expeditions, assisted the orphans of its fallen soldiers only if the mothers agreed to have them raised according to the Anglican faith. Well, for the most part those children were sons of Irish Catholics whom poverty had induced to enlist. After the Crimean War (in which, as we recalled, England, France, and Piedmont fought for the Turkey of the glorious Janissaries and the eunuchs who were made such only if they were baptized), thousands of little Catholics were confined to rigidly Protestant boarding schools. The archbishop of Dublin was the only one to protest, but he found no solidarity among government leaders such as Cavour, who was so sensitive to the news that he received not from London but from Bologna and papal Rome.

In Great Britain itself, moreover (as in the Scandinavian Protestant countries), a law was in force that seriously violated the selfsame authority of parents over their children that was so often invoked for Edgardo Mortara: that is, the state sequestered the children of families that were declared "unbelieving" and therefore were not raising their offspring according to the principles of Anglicanism, the state religion. In order to "deliver them from atheism and error", these little boys, too, ended up in boarding schools run by officials of the Church of England, of which the sovereigns of England were the heads, and therefore, in a way, the popes. The children of the poet Percy B. Shelley met with this fate: they were taken from their father because he was "unbelieving and led a scandalous life" and were reeducated by force according to the official version of Christianity. In Sweden, if a child was not baptized, the authorities saw to it that he was baptized according to the Lutheran rite, and the godparents were designated by the mayor.

The United States was the place where hypocrisy (which is basically a pattern that has marked that great country from the beginning and from which it seems incapable of freeing itself) reached the point of effrontery. Pressured by the 150,000 Jews already on American soil and by Freemasons—of which he was one—President James Buchanan protested through diplomatic channels and asked Pius IX to free little Edgardo. As Kertzer points out:

> His own moral position was not very strong. How could he rail against a government that allowed a child to be forcibly separated from his parents when the same thing happened all the time in the slaveholding portions of his own country?[10]

The millions of black American slaves—like slaves in the Roman Empire—had no authority over their children, and the master could sell the parents to one buyer and the children, even little ones, to another. This terrible situation was denounced in *Uncle Tom's Cabin*, but the "civilized" world was silent about this barbarity; or rather, it put up with denunciations of the horrors of papal theocracy even from America.

[10] Ibid., 127.

Despite the fact that he managed to complete almost nine decades of a life full of labors and great accomplishments, Father Mortara did not enjoy good health. In fact, one reason his life was so meritorious was that—as his confreres wrote in his eulogy—he was able to confront with Christian fortitude and serenity a recurring illness that often condemned him to total inactivity.

There was a nervous component to this illness, but it does not justify the diagnosis of Daniele Scalise, who regards the infirmity as an explicit indictment of the priests and their so-called violence against him. The journalist in psychologist's clothing makes Father Mortara out to be the mentally disturbed prisoner of "his private hell", a disgraced man who walks amid "fogs and troubles" along a path that—even though he is unwilling to admit it—was imposed on him and is nothing but a source of suffering for him. Scalise's interpretation, for all its ambiguous compassion, is unacceptable: it contradicts everything that Mortara wrote about himself, without any hesitation, and the image of an unbalanced man is inconsistent with the practicality, the efficacy, and the enthusiasm of his enormous labors as a pastor, preacher, and builder who saw in his own sufferings a participation in the cross of Christ, for which he was grateful.

The Mortara case, we repeat, was a tragedy that ended by giving great joy to the protagonist, as he himself repeats in his autobiography, but it also caused great sorrow: first of all, for the parents, of course; but also for Pius IX, who—as we recalled—repeatedly told the boy how he had been for him "the son of my tears", because of the campaign of hatred of which he had been the involuntary cause. Nevertheless, it was a drama with a happy ending, an outcome guided by Providence: these are the protagonist's own words, not ours. I emphasize this because I was attacked and insulted when I recounted this story summarily in an article and then in a book, which I concluded by writing: "A dramatic, unique event, in which he seems to see at work a God who can write straight with crooked lines."

If these words are displeasing, your quarrel is not with me but with Father Pio Maria Edgardo, who, throughout his life, never ceased to bless the hand of Anna Morisi that had baptized him and the fortitude of the pope who had defended against everyone and everything his right to be Christian.

I cannot help it if Mortara did not want to "satisfy public opinion", as claimed by the constable who, after Porta Pia, came to the convent where he was living, commanding him to "consider himself liberated" and to return to his family and to his religion, leaving the prison in which the clerics had confined him. The youth not only gave no satisfaction but fled abroad by night because his "liberators" had threatened that if he did not decide to leave Saint Peter in Chains, of which he was very fond, the civil authorities would seize him. This they had already done with another young Roman Jew who was also happy to be preparing for the priesthood (a goal he reached) and who, sequestered by the Piedmontese, was handed over to his family, albeit reluctantly. What did freedom of conscience ever matter in comparison with the political need not to disappoint those who had been moved, or had pretended to be moved, by the tearful story of the little kidnapped boy? In short, this is the heart of the matter, like it or not: we are not the ones who blessed a thousand times the God who was able, in his life, "to write straight with crooked lines"; Mortara was.

But precisely because tragic elements were present, it is also likely that they too were somehow responsible for the nervous component of the canon's recurring illness. The person concerned always spoke openly about his health problems and always attributed them primarily to excessive study: eager to learn as much as possible about the faith that had exploded within him, he neglected his health, which resulted in an exhaustion that unfortunately had lasting consequences.

What is certain is that his sufferings never called into doubt, for him, the goodness of his choice of the Christian life and then of religious life—a choice that was God's more than his own, as he always repeated in the public protests that he was compelled to make when others sought to portray him as a victim. Besides, as we see from the transcript of the trial of his father, Momolo, when he was accused of complicity in murder, disturbances like those that Edgardo complained of were present in other members of the family who had remained in Judaism. Therefore, a hereditary factor should not be ruled out.

It must not be forgotten, however, that Scalise's argument can be turned on its head: the nerves of the religious could have been put to the test not so much by the priests as by their enemies. The extremely harsh anticlerical policy, with its constant harassment, threats, suppressions, and expulsions, with its sarcasms and exiles, made religious life in those decades a Calvary. The Canons Regular, just like their confreres in religion in other orders, were compelled to wander from one country to another, always under the threat of persecution, which was all the fiercer in that it was usually unleashed by ex-priests or former seminarians (such as Émile Combes) who went over to Freemasonry and from there into politics and were morbidly in need of vindicating themselves for their lapses.

Particularly tragic was the moment when Father Mortara fell seriously ill in France, when the umpteenth order of expulsion arrived, for the moment limited to foreign religious. Sick as he was, Mortara would have to travel to Italy. But how could he do that, given that there too all the houses of the order had been suppressed and confiscated (in the Roman monastery where he had spent his happy years at seminary they had settled the faculty of engineering, which is still there), and given that, furthermore, beyond the border an arrest warrant awaited him as a draft dodger, since he had had to flee so as not to be "liberated" by force?

Just then the charismatic figure of Saint John Bosco appeared. He was in France to settle his Salesians there and to raise money. He visited Father Mortara, noticed how serious his illness was, and mystically saw that "a death warrant" hung over him. Yet the young religious had so much to do. He still had to sow and reap much in the Lord's field; therefore, the Lord would grant him many more years of life. So Don Bosco said; and so, of course, it happened.

It was no accident that for the rest of his life Father Pio Maria considered himself the recipient of a miracle by that great saint. In 1867, when he was only sixteen years old and still a novice in Rome, he had had the honor and the joy of serving Mass for him. Don Bosco spoke with him afterward and rejoiced in his fervor. As he said good-bye Don Bosco informed Edgardo that when he returned to Turin he would write to him to communicate something important that he did not want to tell him in conversation. Indeed, a few days later the letter arrived from Valdocco; it said that over the boy's head he had seen "an ominous dark cloud". But standing above it were "two angels holding a beautiful crown of flaming roses". The

saint deduced from this a blessed eternity for that unexpected son of the Church, but the finish line would be
reached by way of many tribulations. And they did arrive
punctually, starting with the sufferings because of his pre-
carious health.

As a believer (and, of course, I do not claim that someone who is not should agree) and as a devotee of Don
Bosco—a devotee who is often taken aback by his mysterious charisms that were always confirmed by later events—
I draw two conclusions from this: the authenticity, if not
the heroism, of Father Mortara's commitment, to the point
of meriting for him an eternal crown; and the role of the
sickness that accompanied him for many years, which was
foreseen, willed, and therefore providential.

But now, finally, let us let him speak; otherwise we too
run the risk of getting wrapped up in our own chatter,
without listening to him. Let us listen to him, after we
make just a few final remarks.

First of all, it will sometimes appear that Father Mortara
is excessively severe in judging his time, making neither
allowances nor concessions for its positions. It could not
be otherwise, since in all things he wanted to be the faithful son of the pope who, in his *Syllabus*, thundered against
the present and future errors of a culture that had declared
war on the Church. Even though he died when World
War II had already begun, our religious is a Catholic
of the nineteenth century and still carries about with him
the zeal and the wounds of that century. He is intransigent, to be sure, with a passionate temperament and
therefore polemical. But we must not forget the situation
of the Church in 1888, in which the still young religious
composed these autobiographical notes. Discriminated
against in Protestant and Orthodox countries, persecuted

in Catholic lands, attacked by liberalism, scientism, and socialism, the "little flock" of Catholics felt that it was in a fortress under siege. Whether out of hatred or disdain, their faith was called "papism", and its very right to exist was called into question.

Another precaution: someone who wants to write history, or even just an honest, accurate chronicle, must judge the protagonists of the events not according to his own times and perspectives, but according to theirs. One example among many: Mortara relates that once, when he had put his dearest father Pius IX in danger of falling through his youthful emotion and carelessness, the pope asked him to kiss the floor and then to make the Sign of the Cross on it with his tongue. This was an exercise of obedience and humility (which was rather widely used then, and not only in Catholic boarding schools but also, for example, in the exclusive Anglican schools), after which the pope blessed his pupil. The latter, I repeat it again here, was very grateful to him for this penance, accepting it as a further act of love for him, an invaluable call to the virtues of a religious.

In contrast, there are some, such as Daniele Scalise and others, who, while claiming to do the work of historians, speak about "an episode of the utmost cruelty" and about "the repulsive brutality of such a papal gesture". Such judgments totally lack an understanding for the Catholic perspective. Indeed, similar instances of indignation are based on the "feelings" of a contemporary layman who takes his own little era as an absolute standard and claims to judge the outlook of nineteenth-century religious life (and also of every century, including ours), for which the virtue of obedience to one's superior is rooted in the obedience owed to the Almighty. Over two millennia a surprisingly rich theology of religious obedience has been developed, and for someone truly acquainted with it, it is quite consistent with the spirit of Scripture.

Therefore, only a simpleton or a sectarian can speak about "cruelty" and "brutality" in reference to an order that, by combining sacred obedience and Christian humility, was in reality pedagogically appropriate—as Mortara himself acknowledged with gratitude. It is no accident that he decided to record the episode when he was called on to testify in the process for the beatification of Pius IX. What for some might be a disgrace, for the Church is an act that witnesses to the gospel as it ought to be lived out in religious life, in which obedience is the first of the virtues and the vows required of the candidate.

A third and final precaution: his contemporaries tell us what an extraordinary orator Father Mortara was, in all the many languages that he mastered. Ardent in his faith, yet not forgetting the *rational reasons* for it (he was a solidly trained theologian), he did not hesitate to appeal also to the *reasons of the heart*, eliciting tears and conversions in the crowds that flocked to hear him. We know from countless witnesses that hearing him proclaim the Gospels by which he lived was an experience they never forgot.

Although he spoke powerfully from the pulpit, he seems not to have been equally adept at writing. Consequently he did not leave us any books, but only a few short works or the occasional transcription of one of his masterly speeches. Therefore, in the text that we present (which, as I said, Mortara wrote in the third person), we should not look for literary value or the skill of a professional writer. These pages were not written as the rules of good literature would dictate.

But so what? They have a documentary value: in response to so many distortions, they intend to clarify how things really happened. They are, first and foremost, a testimony, the record, as it were, of a unique adventure. The adventure of a Jewish boy, over whom a pope, an emperor, the king, ministers, ambassadors, bankers, leaders of the press and of the judiciary, cardinals, Freemasons, theologians, and rabbis clashed. As he was dying in foggy Wallonia (Belgium), while Hitler's Wehrmacht was massing at the borders, he summarized his life as follows: "I had only one goal, I nurtured only one desire: to give glory to God, to edify souls, to pray that everyone—starting with my Jewish brethren, whom I love so much—might recognize in Jesus the divine Redeemer."

POSTSCRIPT

While I was finishing my review of the printer's proofs, I found in one of the usual packages of books sent to me by editors one by John Cornwell, senior research fellow at Jesus College in Cambridge and writer of editorials for major English-language newspapers. He calls himself Catholic and assures his readers that he criticizes the Church with the interest and emotion of someone who considers it his home. His latest book, *The Pope in Winter*, is about the "winter", that is, the final stage, of John Paul II's life.[1]

The reason I decided to add this postscript is that I do not want to deprive the reader of the latest discovery, the fruit of the research and reflections of a Catholic historian of this ilk. The true origin of the Mortara case, he says, is the fact that Pius IX "today, in any civil society, would have faced a jail sentence for child molestation and kidnap". This pope, Cornwell assures his readers, was a sort of precursor of the American priests now being tried for pedophilia. Indeed, he was notorious for "the abuse of minors". The future Blessed, we learn, had "a mawkish and unlawful relationship with the boy". Cornwell claims to have proof and accuses the nineteenth-century pope of "hiding [Mortara] under his cassock in a way that today would be described as 'inappropriate'".

I admit that my ingenuity is such that I had never thought of that motive for the famous incident! I had indeed read,

[1] John Cornwell, *The Pope in Winter: The Dark Face of John Paul's Papacy* (New York: Viking, 2004).

in Mortara's deposition also for the process of beatification of his spiritual father, an anecdote in which, in my innocence, I had not noticed anything sordid.

It is necessary to know that, in keeping with the extroverted, good-natured character of that pope and with the Romans' sincere affection for him, Pius IX liked to take a walk through the city in the evening before supper. Accompanied only by his secretary and a prelate, without any trace of gendarmes, he used to stroll through the streets of the central district; he would greet and converse with those who wished to speak with him or entrust a petition to him; he would make a witty remark (all historians highlight his geniality and good sense of humor). To give a sense of these daily walks: One day he saw a boy crying in front of a tall gate. Upon inquiring he learned that the boy had been sent by his parents to buy a bottle of wine and had stumbled. The bottle broke, and the wine spilled on the pavement, and the boy did not dare to go back home. Passersby then saw the pope personally enter the nearest wine shop, take out his purse, pay for a bottle of Castelli white, and hand it over to the weeping boy.

Now, having understood that story, here is one involving Edgardo, who was taking his walk as a novice with the Canons Regular. Pius IX, noticing his protégé, called to him, asked him the news about his studies, and then, while conversing with other persons and pretending to lose interest in him, wrapped him with his big red cloak. Then, turning around to the bystanders, he asked in a tone that was half-worried, half-vexed: "Edgardo? Where has Edgardo gone? That young rascal, I wanted to say good-bye, and he has disappeared!" Immediately afterward he opened his cape: "Ah, there he is! Now what have you got yourself into?" Of course, everyone laughed, and the boy was so amused by the little joke that the pope repeated it several times when he met him again on the street.

The historian and instructor at Jesus College in Cambridge claims that here we are looking at obvious "sexual molestation" and unspeakable "abuse of minors", which today would land someone in prison. If Pius IX "ignored the pleas of the world, including no fewer than twenty editorials in the *New York Times*, to give the child back to his parents", as Cornwell informs us, it was because the licentious old man did not want to break off his "unlawful relationship" with the little boy.

There is more: the pope, again according to Cornwell, must have procured his young sexual prey through a network of characters like himself. Indeed, he informs us, the papal police were tipped off and "turned up in the parents' absence". In Rome this was a signal used by old pederasts ("The little boy is alone!"), and so the hired ruffians arrived and hauled him off to the degenerate who was already slobbering in the Vatican. The indignant conclusion of the historian, referring to Pius IX's beatification: "A fine exemplar for the twenty-first century, to be sure!"

This beatification is invalid, according to the British professor who apparently knows canon law better than the pope—because "there had been no public cult of Pope Pius IX (a prerequisite for beatification). On the contrary, following his death a Roman crowd had attempted to throw his cadaver into the Tiber while it was being drawn to its final resting place."

The scholar proves himself ignorant, therefore, of the fact that upon the death of Pius IX, in February 1878, the crowd that went to Saint Peter's, where the body lay in state uninterruptedly for three days and three nights, was so large that the religious authorities, in order to avoid incidents and to maintain order among the devotees, did what it had never intended to do. Notwithstanding the indignant determination with which the Vatican had closed its doors to those whom it considered "Piedmontese invaders", the cardinals in charge during the *sede vacante* (vacancy in the See of Peter) were compelled to request the intervention of the Italian troops. It took a whole regiment on the square and inside the basilica to make the approximately three hundred thousand people file past in an orderly fashion. (Rome then had a population of a little more than two hundred thousand; the others arrived from all the surrounding regions or from abroad.) Throughout the world there was a flourish of monuments, busts, and plaques in honor of the deceased pontiff; and his successor, Leo XIII, received requests for his beatification, signed by hundreds of bishops and thousands of the faithful.

The general response, therefore, was not rejection but, on the contrary, veneration. Additional impressive testimony of it was the scuffle around the bier that Cornwell alludes to—which, according to him, showed the hostile sentiments of the Romans. In reality, the citizens greatly alarmed the Italian authorities—who were still insecure in their control over the city, a rule that many thought would be temporary—by filling with candles the windowsills of the houses on the night of July 13, 1881, when the coffin of Pius IX was carried to San Lorenzo al Verano, where he had wished to be laid to rest. According to the thoroughly reliable reports of the police, at least one hundred thousand persons, despite the hour, followed the coffin, carrying torches and tapers. At the entrance to the bridge over the Tiber, the funeral escort was attacked by a group of about three hundred troublemakers, political extremists and common hooligans, incited, according to many testimonies, by a deputy who was drunk (as often happened), the famous Felice Cavallotti, leader of the radical left. They tried to take possession of the coffin so as to throw it into the river but were scattered by the reaction of the crowd of devotees.

These are the facts, and they clearly show how representative of "the Romans" those troublemakers were; in fact, in quite a few cases they were common delinquents, as proved by the arrests made by the *Regia Questura* (Royal Police).

For Professor John Cornwell, however, there is no doubt: the beatification of this dubious pedophile, execrated by everybody and venerated by no one, is proof that John Paul II was already incapable of making sound judgments during the Jubilee Year 2000. Only a pope who was out of his mind could think of proposing for the veneration of the Church one of his predecessors who went so far as to kidnap boys, Jewish ones to boot, in order to abuse them sexually.

What can we say? Nothing, except to confirm what we said at the start: the Mortara case is still with us. Reconstructing how things really happened is, for any honest person, a duty of truth and justice. Giovanni Maria Mastai Ferretti and Pio Maria Edgardo Mortara (together with John Paul II) deserve much better than historians like John Cornwell—the latest example, for now, in a series of journalists who too often are as reliable as he is.

With that I thought I was finished. Instead I had to reopen the computer file to confirm once again how inexhaustible the sectarian use of the Mortara case is. It is just as inexhaustible as the anti-Catholic hatred that thrives in the United States, where, among other things, the Ku Klux Klan, having spent, so to speak, its vitriol against blacks, was refounded in 1915 by a Protestant pastor with the primary task of combating the "papists".

A reader to whom I had mentioned the topic I was writing about informed me of the appearance of a comic book by Marvel, one of the largest publishers of that genre in America (and worldwide). The storyline is credited not to an anonymous employee but rather to a famous novelist who had an idea: situate the Mortara case in seventeenth-century Spain and England, so as to portray the horrors of the Inquisition at its height and to show, in contrast, how much more presentable the Reformation was, Anglican-style. The series, composed of eight issues, depicts a little Jewish boy kidnapped from an Italian ghetto. And by whom? By pedophile priests, of course. Since the prey "is a handsome boy, for a Jew" (as his kidnapper says), the pope, too, takes advantage of him and then refuses to return him to his desperate parents. Furthermore, the prelates respond with an unmistakable double meaning: "We have taken him, and we have made him ours." The clerical homosexual community is unwilling to give up this dainty they have acquired. The comic-strip pontiff declares, with the usual hypocritical cynicism, that if he were to give him back to his people, he would "condemn him to hell".

But if, as we see, pederasty seems to have become the new trope for interpreting the Mortara case, there is a significant innovation in the Marvel comic books. The little Jewish boy "taken" by the lecherous priests will have his revenge: He agrees to become a religious but conceals his hatred for the Church in order to climb the rungs of an ecclesiastical career. Having become grand inquisitor, of all things, he takes advantage of his position to promote the enemies of the Catholic Church secretly. When discovered, he is sentenced by his confreres to be burned at the stake, even though he will then be saved by the intervention of superheroes like Spider-Man, the X-Men, and Captain America.

This is a significant innovation. Indeed, you do not have to be a psychologist to guess the more or less unconscious motive: that is, reacting to disappointment with the "real" Mortara's choice and insinuating that he only pretended to accept the Church and to love the pope and in reality hated them and wanted to destroy them. So say the cartoons of Marvel Comics in the United States.

THE MORTARA CHILD AND PIUS IX

The Autobiographical Account of
the "Mortara Case"
Written by the Protagonist,
Reverend Father Pio Maria Mortara, C.R.L.

The Baptism

Edgardo Levi Mortara was born in Bologna, the capital of the legation by the same name and of the province of Romagna, belonging to the Papal States, on August 21, 1851. He was the ninth of twelve children from the lawful marriage of Salomone Levi Mortara with Marianna Padovani. His parents professed the Jewish religion, and they were very faithful to their beliefs and to the requirements of the Law of Moses.

The civil laws then in force in the Papal States strictly forbade Jews to have Catholic servants in their households or at their service. This law intended, first of all, to protect the Jews themselves, so that incidents like the one that happened to the Mortaras (albeit by a providential decree) would not occur.

Against the civil law, therefore, Edgardo's parents had in their house a young woman named Anna Morisi for the domestic services necessary to the family on Saturday, which is sacred and holy for the people of Israel, a day on which any kind of work or material occupation is strictly prohibited. She would become, in Heaven's hands, the instrument and channel of grace for Edgardo. The child, in fact, was just a little over one year old when he was struck by a terrible disease, accompanied by raging fevers, which in a few days put his life in great danger.

The progress of the illness was so rapid that it did not take long for clear signs of an imminent tragedy to appear. Given the extreme pallor, the hollowed eyes, and the loss of appetite that he presented, the doctors had lost all hope of saving him. His disconsolate parents, given over to the deepest sorrow, did not leave the cradle except out of necessity. Especially inconsolable was his afflicted mother, who wept profusely.

In such tragic circumstances, Anna Morisi, the young servant previously mentioned, remembered what the doctrine of the Church teaches: namely, that is lawful for any Christian to administer Baptism to a child who is thought to be near death. She then waited for a moment when the disconsolate parents left the cradle. Then, following the instructions received from some neighbors, she took a glass of water (consistent with the account that the servant gave in court under oath) and gave the dying child the saving water *per aspersionem*, according to the method for Baptism of the sick.

Once she had performed this act (in the presence of no other witnesses except God and His angels), which was apparently so simple, but in reality so great and with transcendent consequences, Anna felt very comforted. She thought, as she was to say later, that with that act she would send to Paradise a poor child whom she dearly loved.

However, by a divine arrangement, the girl's fears did not materialize. After the child's soul was regenerated, incorporated into Christ, and made an heir to heavenly glory, thanks to the sacrament, supernatural life gleamed

and redounded on his frail, distressed constitution. Therefore, he gradually regained strength, and finally his health
was completely restored.

It is impossible to describe the joy of the afflicted parents,
in contrast to the agitation that took possession of the servant. Seeing that the child survived the illness, she realized
the disturbing consequences that would follow because
of the Baptism, which was unknown to the parents.

What was she supposed to do? Reveal everything? To
whom? To the parents, who were so profoundly faithful
to their religion? What would be the consequences for
her? What fury, what hatred, what mistreatments would
she have to bear? And what about poor Edgardo? What
would become of him? In short, poor Anna did not have
the courage to state the facts and so remained silent—a
silence that was fatal and lamentable for the boy, as understandable as it was on the girl's part.

This, though, is how the infinite mercy of God came to
realize its purpose, in its maternal predilection for Edgardo:
five years after the child's Baptism, one of his little brothers, named Aristide, became seriously ill and was on the
point of death. Guessing Anna's thought and desire, her
friends reminded her that it was impossible for her not to
baptize the poor little boy, whom the doctors had already
given up for dead.

To their great surprise, she told them that she did not
dare to do it, so as not to find herself in a second painful
predicament. "Why?" her friends asked.

"Because I fear", Anna said, "that this child too may
survive his Baptism, as it happened to Edgardo, who has
been a baptized Christian for five years now, without anyone knowing it, not even him."

"What!" the frightened women retorted. "Do you realize what you are saying? Do you dare to remain silent?"

"I do not have the courage to tell what I did; I prefer to resign myself to the deep sorrow caused by my silence." To this, her friends replied that she could tell her confessor, who would then be responsible for bringing the secret to the attention of the competent authority.

This was exactly what Anna did; meanwhile, she was careful not to baptize little Aristide. This boy, more unfortunate than Edgardo, succumbed in a short time to the disease. His death was the accidental and indirect cause of a future that in itself was full of terrible conflicts and bitter struggles, but for Edgardo a very fortunate and happy one.

The separation

When Anna's confessor had learned what had happened, and with the penitent's consent to communicate the whole matter to the competent authority, the reverend Archbishop of Bologna, His Eminence Michele Cardinal Viale Prelà, was informed. Wasting no time, he spoke about it with the Most Reverend Father Pier Gaetano Feletti, president of the second tribunal of the Inquisition. In agreement with him, he reported the happening to the Sacred Congregation of the Penitentiary, whose Cardinal Prefect informed His Holiness, the Supreme Pontiff Pius IX, of holy and blessed memory.

This glorious, immortal Pope, who will live forever in the memory and heart of the Catholic world, acted in this matter guided by one of those immediate insights into truth and by one of those secret inspirations that will be made known sooner or later, when we will see the halo of the saints shining on his illustrious forehead. Without hesitation, he ordered the Archbishop of Bologna to give Father Feletti a delicate assignment. Employing all possible means of persuasion, he was to make it clear to Edgardo's parents that the Church had the duty and the unavoidable obligation to take charge of the child's religious education. In fact, by a very obvious intervention of Providence, without anyone interfering in it, he had received the Sacrament of Baptism and had therefore been incorporated into Christ and His heavenly flock. So as not to impose any burden on the parents, the Pope himself would provide the necessary resources for the child's education, supporting him at his own expense in a Catholic boarding school in Bologna. That way, his parents would be able to visit him whenever they wanted.

When the orders from the Supreme Pontiff were communicated to the Archbishop, the latter entrusted the execution of them to Father Feletti, who did not delay in conveying them to the Mortaras, showing up in person at their house. The response, after the revelation by the above-mentioned priest, was a violent explosion of sorrow and a torrent of tears, especially from the child's mother. The cleric did not dare to insist on that occasion. He then returned to the house several times, without getting any result, since the child's father was absolutely and intransigently opposed to any kind of separation, even in the more mitigated form, while the mother would burst into tears. All the means and resources of persuasion and conciliation that the inquisitor employed proved to be useless.

The Supreme Pontiff Pius IX, informed about the turn that the matter was taking, ordered that Signor and Signora Mortara be reminded once again that the Catholic Church could not fail to carry out such a sacred duty. If the means of persuasion were not enough, he would see himself obliged, as Vicar of Christ and temporal Prince, to take other measures, albeit with the utmost sorrow and deploring to the highest degree the sad consequences. The child's parents themselves would then be the only ones responsible for them. Indeed, they had exposed themselves to these painful predicaments because they had failed to comply with the laws of the Papal States, which (as we explained) strictly forbade the Jews to hire Christian domestic servants. Now they could certainly accept the consolation that was being offered to them—the plan to put the child in a Catholic boarding school right there in Bologna (until he reached of the age of majority).

All of this was communicated by Father Feletti to the Mortaras, but he met the same intransigence, while the parents' sorrow and anger increased and were manifested more and more vehemently. There was nothing left to do but wait for the supreme decision of Pius IX, not only as Head of the Church and Vicar of Christ, but also as temporal Prince in charge of enforcing the laws then in effect.

Meanwhile, the Jewish community in Bologna—where there was no ghetto, in other words, no separate district for the Jews, a circumstance that was entirely in their favor—took a decidedly hostile attitude toward the papal orders. This community got the entire hierarchy of the synagogues involved in its protest, so that Signor Mortara was persuaded to oppose categorically the proposals from the authorities, no matter what conditions were formulated.

This opposition party kept on growing, swelling, as usually happens in such circumstances, to include the whole group of openly hostile people mixed in with the Jewish community residing in Bologna. Such people, dissatisfied and clamoring for reforms in the Papal States, echoed the Jews. On one side, therefore, were the restless souls who dreamed of a regime of absolute freedom; on the other, the mass of the timid and the cowardly who did not have the courage to oppose the revolt of suspicious individuals and withdrew into a silence that was not free of culpable solidarity.

That being the case, it was obvious that this minority of rebels, in which Jews and Catholics attached to the deadly principles of modern naturalism united, would never have allowed the least intervention of the ecclesiastical authority in the case of the Mortara child, judging the matter, without hesitation, in favor of the parents. Those rioters boasted that they were defending the family against the injustices and outrages—so they said—of the despotic power of the popes. Therefore they did not hesitate to proclaim that they would openly oppose the resolute measures that, by necessity, the papal government had taken. They soon prepared for resistance and even for bloody clashes.

When all this was brought to the attention of the Supreme Pontiff, the following plan was outlined. It was to proceed with the separation of the child, a sad but necessary measure that was entrusted to the executive power. This is how they intended to thwart the resistance of the adverse party and to ensure the success of the operation. The purpose was to save the soul of the Mortara child from perversion and violent, compulsory apostasy, in defense of the Church's rights, which are the very rights of God. This was the plan that Father Feletti carried out by the express order of Pius IX.

In 1859, as a result of the deadly insurgency of the province of Romagna and the arrival there of the Piedmontese government, which hypocritically boasted that it had restored the order that it had in fact troubled, a usurping government was established violently. Thus began the sacrilegious dethronement of the Supreme Pontiff Pius IX (even though he was still recognized as the rightful sovereign by the majority of the people of Romagna), and the secularization of the Papal States was partially achieved.

On that occasion the Most Reverend Father Feletti, still Inquisitor General, was arrested in his room while in his own bed at three o'clock in the morning. He was taken to jail as a precaution, accused, and denounced as the one immediately and directly responsible for the abduction of the Mortara child. A trial was prepared, but the above-mentioned priest was acquitted and released after three months of detention. The version of his court-appointed lawyer triumphed, stating that Father Feletti was *not responsible*, because he had done nothing but carry out the strict orders he had received from his rightful superior, the Roman Pontiff, the one chiefly responsible for the abduction. In Rome, with great pleasure and tears in his eyes, Father Feletti hugged the Mortara child, for whose eternal salvation he had suffered so much, and he always showed a special affection for him. Father Mortara will always hold very dear the memory of this respectable friar, who was one of those who more closely intervened in the spiritual regeneration and rehabilitation of his soul.

To return to our story: one day in June 1858, Edgardo woke up between two guards who had appeared late at night at his father's house, to keep the boy from being taken away while preparations were made for the separation.

It is easy to imagine the terror of the poor little creature when he saw himself flanked by the guards, as he had always shown great fear at the sight of a soldier. The military men, who treated the family members in the most conciliatory and benevolent way possible, never left Edgardo for a moment; they always accompanied him to every room of the house to which he had to go. In those days the mother, Marianna, with some of her children, had retreated to a house in the countryside, while Edgardo stayed with his father and the other siblings.

At last, the peremptory order arrived from Rome. On June 24, at nightfall, the chief of police and two guards on horseback arrived at the Mortara house to attend to the separation before daybreak.

The mother, Marianna, had returned home earlier, to give the child one last hug. The disconsolate lady, despite all the advice given to her, preferred to risk a serious incident rather than to let Edgardo leave without saying goodbye to him.

Finally the time of separation arrived. The father again protested vehemently against the act, which he described as barbaric, while the mother burst into sighs, tears, and piercing cries. Truly the mother was in a pitiful state: as she gave a last hug to Edgardo, she was completely bathed in tears. Succumbing to the intensity of her sorrow, she fainted and fell to the ground. Her husband and the other children lifted her back up. Everybody wept bitterly.

Edgardo does not recall having cried a lot. He does remember the following fact. When one of the guards took him in his arms to carry him to the carriage that was waiting in front of the door to the house, he asked with simple candor: "And now, are you going to cut off my head?" After a few kind words from the guards, he calmed down and put up no resistance.

They put him in the carriage in the middle of three guards; gendarmes on horseback provided the escort. They spread a coat over him so that he could rest. The night was indeed very chilly. After leaving his father's house, seeing that he was among soldiers and strangers, the child began to cry. He called loudly, shouting for his parents.

The guards talked to him in a friendly way; they gave him little cakes and chocolates. A great calm, a deep, peaceful sleep then followed those first upsetting moments.

The guards had been ordered to wear uniforms, to command respect for the authorities and to protect against possible riots. Once outside the place of the sequestration, at the city gates, the guards in uniform left Edgardo. Only a corporal wearing civilian clothes remained with him, out of consideration for the natural discomfort that the child felt toward anything military. The traveling companion had strict orders to treat the child with great kindness and benevolence, lavishing on him all sorts of attention and care, and he did this very conscientiously. Edgardo, though, did not always reciprocate the solicitude of his faithful, loyal guide, sometimes giving in to a surge of ill humor caused by the memory of the parents whom he had just abandoned. He put up resistance when they were about to enter a Catholic church. He gave in only when the guard gave him some coins. He was even not respectful to the guard but let loose and gave him a little slap on the face. This act proves the bad instincts of the child and gives a glimpse of what he would have become if the infinite mercy of God had not chosen him precisely at the moment when he was approaching the age of reason.

Usually, though, Edgardo did not manifest a rebellious character. Two very religious ladies who were traveling with him realized what was happening. They offered to introduce him to the basics of Christian doctrine. Edgardo gladly accepted and learned to recite the Our Father and the Hail Mary, to make the Sign of the Cross, and to invoke Mary Most Holy. Those good ladies, whom Edgardo will never forget, were the first to continue the motherly care of God's Church for the child's benefit—care that had started with the blessed hand of the girl who, in the supernatural order, can be called the mother of Edgardo.

The Mortara child and Pius IX

The separation had taken place on June 24, the feast of Saint John the Baptist. On the twenty-ninth of that month, the feast of the Holy Apostles Peter and Paul, Edgardo arrived in Rome. He was entrusted, by order of the Supreme Pontiff, to Don Enrico Sarra, rector of the Institute for Neophytes, or new converts. He intended to welcome him into his own house, offering him all that he needed. His sisters Natalia and Anna proved to be very diligent, taking charge especially of the child's religious education.

The first thing Don Sarra did was to introduce Edgardo to His Holiness. Inspired by the words of Saint Paul to the Corinthians: "Gratia Dei sum id quod sum" (By the Grace of God I am what I am), Don Sarra explained to the child the sentiments of filial gratitude toward the Supreme Pontiff that the child ought to nurture.

Pius IX received him with the utmost kindness. Hearing from his lips the exact words that the rector had taught him, the Holy Father was deeply moved and tenderly embraced the child. He told him that, even though it had been sadly but absolutely necessary to separate him from his parents, he, the universal father of the faithful, adopted him from that moment on as his son, taking charge of his education and ensuring his future. Then he gave him a beautiful statue of Saint Agnes, which Edgardo preserved as a treasure. When he dismissed him, he embraced him again, blessing him with all the tenderness and affection of a father.

From that moment on, the blessings of Pius IX never abandoned the child. They earned him the obvious help of Divine Providence. They allowed him not to succumb to the terrible struggle that Hell was preparing for him, making use of his own family.

Indeed, after Edgardo's arrival in Rome and after he was strengthened by the very affectionate blessings of Pius IX, the child's parents arrived in the capital. They got out of their carriage in front of the main door of the Institute for

Neophytes, loudly demanding to be permitted to see and embrace their child.

Although Don Sarra foresaw the consequences of this meeting and the danger to which the little boy was exposed, he nevertheless did not forbid it. He presented Edgardo to his parents in the lobby of the institute. He himself attended the meeting after the entrance of several guards (to prevent any sort of deplorable incident).

In that setting the same scenes were repeated as in Bologna: the mother was distraught with sorrow; the father uttered threats. He swore that Edgardo would surely return to his family.

The parents stayed in Rome for a whole month, visiting the child every day in the rector's house. They were always accompanied by the Chief Rabbi of the synagogue. They resorted to every expedient and trick to conquer Edgardo's perseverance. Making use of very enticing promises, they sought to convince him to go back home with them.

Later on we will say what the young neophyte's attitude was when faced with those attempts by his parents, who gained nothing.

Don Sarra never left the child alone with his parents. A month after their arrival, the parents left. The mother returned to Bologna, while the father remained nearby, looking for some favorable opportunity to succeed in his intentions.

Edgardo was taken to the suburban city of Alatri to spend a few days with the Sarra family. One day, while Edgardo was leaving a church with a priest for whom he had just served Mass, his father appeared in order to carry the child off.

Great fear came over the boy, but a priest, Don Vincenzo Sarra, brother of the rector, arrived immediately. Don Vincenzo reprimanded Signor Mortara very vehemently, so that the latter went away. He did not appear again until 1870, a time that we will discuss later.

In the meantime, since another abduction attempt was feared, His Excellency Monsignor Gaetano Rodilossi, the Bishop of that city, welcomed Edgardo into his palace, lavishing on him, in the name of Pius IX, all sorts of courtesies and considerations.

The time was drawing near, however, when the angelic and imperturbable Pope of the Immaculate would promote the work of God's infinite mercy by offering His protégé a Catholic education in one of the many colleges of the Eternal City.

Here is how Divine Providence intervened so that Edgardo would be entrusted by Pope Pius IX to the Canons Regular of the Lateran. Don Sarra's good sisters used to attend the Basilica of Saint Peter in Chains, which had been staffed by those Canons since the days of Julius II. They brought little Edgardo with them.

The habit of the Canons Regular is a white cassock, and over it a *rocchetto*, a white linen surplice, which they always wear, so the Roman people familiarly call them "Rocchettini". It was the custom in the times to which we refer to give the students of the colleges in Rome run by the Canons Regular the same habit as the religious (as the Benedictines and other orders did), with a slight modification to distinguish them from the teachers.

As he attended Mass in that venerable basilica, and saw that snow-white habit worn with such modesty by those priests, and also by those innocent, simple boys, Edgardo was deeply impressed. He showed a keen desire to be admitted to that college and be clothed in the same angelic habit.

As soon as His Holiness was informed of the child's desire, he ordered him to be welcomed in that place.

On December 8, 1858, as they played the last chimes announcing the Solemn Mass in honor of the Immaculate Virgin, the adopted son, the protégé of Pius IX, climbed the slopes of the Esquiline Hill. He was accompanied by Don Sarra, who entrusted him, on behalf of His Holiness, to the Reverend Father Bardagni, Abbot of Saint Peter in Chains and superior of the community. He welcomed the child with great affection, immediately commending him to the *maestro*, or prefect, of the students. Young Edgardo took his place among them to begin his studies of Latin.

The special blessings and paternal affection of the Supreme Pontiff never abandoned Edgardo for a single moment, as was evident in various circumstances. He sent him gifts; he conversed with him and embraced him tenderly when he met him walking with the other pupils, covering him with his big red cape. He blessed him effusively, speaking very kindly to him. He never failed to confirm the right and the duty that he had, as Vicar of Christ, to save the soul of this child, who had cost the blood of God.

One cannot help weeping at the memory of such benevolent yet energetic words coming from the mouth of the Supreme Pontiff, when he saw before him the child for whose salvation (as we will see) he was to suffer much distress and bitterness.

Pius IX stated more forcefully than ever the rights of the Church, Mother of all the faithful, on the occasion of the solemn Te Deum that was sung every year on April 12. That day was the anniversary of the miraculous preservation of the life of the august Pontiff; he could have died in the collapse of the floor in a hall where a reception was being held in his honor. The Te Deum was offered in one of the rooms of the residence of the Canons Regular, adjacent to the Church of Saint Agnes Outside the

Walls. There, Pius IX, returning from a visit to the Cat-
acombs of Saint Alexander, was resting a little, while the
large crowd was admitted for the ceremony of the kissing
of the holy foot.

On that day, young Edgardo greeted the Supreme Pontiff with a poem. Pius IX was deeply moved and could not
help weeping. On one of these occasions, the great Pontiff
exclaimed: "The great and the lowly have done everything
possible. Resorting to all sorts of expedients and tricks, to
the press and diplomacy, all the governments of the Old
and the New World united and conspired to take away
from me, from Christ, and from His Church, the soul of
this child, whom you see here kneeling at my feet. I do not
feel sorry, though, for what I have done on his behalf, to
save a soul that cost the blood of God. On the contrary, I
ratify and confirm everything. Protesting against these vain
efforts, I declare to everyone that not even all the bayonets
of the world will force me to hand this child over to the
clutches of the Revolution and the devil."

These and similar words by the Holy Pontiff will never
be erased from the memory and the heart of the lucky
child. Confused and absorbed by the feeling of his own
unworthiness, he will never tire of marveling at "altitu-
dinem consilii divini super salutem generis humani" (the
sublimity of God's plan for the salvation of mankind), in
the words of Saint Augustine. In fact, he thought that all
that he could do or suffer would be nothing in return for
such a great grace.

Journalism and diplomacy in the case of the Mortara child

It is not my intention to dwell on an explanation of the beginnings, the developments, and the conclusion of the

enormous campaign that was organized by the press and the diplomatic corps because of the Mortara issue, or case. On the one hand, it is known to everybody; on the other hand, modern history will fully satisfy anyone who wants to inquire about it. I will frankly say that, having arrived at this point of my story, I cannot help but feel a deep sadness. In fact, I see the Catholic consciousness hindered and trampled nowadays to the point of completely forgetting even the most basic rudiments of Faith.

Thanks to the tricks and the machinations of the Arians, the Second Council of Ephesus was named by Saint Jerome, in his energetic and inimitable style, the Robber Council of Ephesus. The Great Doctor exclaimed: "The Catholic world was astonished to see itself suddenly become Arian." Similarly, referring to the sad spectacle that press and statesmanship would present in the Mortara case, one might say with Louis Veuillot (of whom we must speak later) that the Catholic world was astonished, recognizing that it had forgotten Christian doctrine and no longer knew what Baptism was.

As Dom Prosper Guéranger, Abbot of Solesmes, remarked very pertinently, naturalism had taken possession of society. Over its eyes it had placed a thick veil that did not allow it to see or understand what was obvious and indisputable even for a seven-year-old.

In Italy, as in France, Germany, Spain, and Austria, in Rome, and even in Asia and Africa, in the Old as well in the New World, in the press, in parliaments, courts, theaters, casinos, cafés, lounges, and clubs, the learned and the ignorant, believers and unbelievers, the great and the lowly (as Pius IX remarked), men of all kinds, of all beliefs and convictions would state their opinion. They meddled and lifted their voices in a horrible uproar, in a dizzying turmoil. The central, red-hot engine of this revolt was the press of every stripe and affiliation. It reflected the troublesome state of people's minds and of society.

Truly we can say with Dante in his *Inferno*: "Different languages, horrible dialects, / Words of pain, accents of wrath. / Loud, hoarse voices and with them the sound of hands clapping."

This agitation, this convulsive movement that was at work in the press and in public opinion apparently seemed to correspond to a centrifugal trend. In reality, it obeyed a centralizing impulse that came from France and returned to it. Everything revolved around the great Caesar of the era, the great Constellation of the diplomatic heavens, the arbiter of the destiny of the official world, the god of rulers—in short, around Napoleon III. His name was enough to impose respect, to silence the shouting, to calm the agitation. In him was concentrated, more than in the oracle of Greek philosophy, all the solemn and oppressive force of the famous and apodictic motto: "Ipse dixit. Napoleon locutus est, causa finita est." (He himself said it. Napoleon has spoken; the matter is settled.)

All eyes then turned toward France and were fixed on the Caesar of Paris. England, a Protestant nation, had already ruled on the Mortara case, as was to be expected, not at all in favor of "popery", through the famous Lord Palmerston, Prime Minister of the government of Queen Victoria. All the other Protestant nations then agreed with Lord Palmerston.

In those regions where Catholicism was dominant, two parties quickly formed. The first was made up of loyal Catholics, defenders of the Supreme Pontiff. The other consisted of freethinkers, enemies of the Church and the papacy. The latter condemned Pius IX and, using the issue as a pretext, loudly demanded the introduction of reforms that they said were necessary in the Papal States.

In Spain, the newspaper *La Esperanza*, edited by the Señores Hoz and Vildósola, openly supported the orthodox Catholic doctrine, forcefully responding to the direct attacks on the incomparable Pontiff, in defense of the Church's rights.

In Italy, where Pius IX was still King and Pontiff, Catholic convictions were manifested more energetically in response to protests and confused rumors orchestrated by Masonic sects and by clubs that were protected by the government of the king of Sardinia Vittorio Emanuele II, led by Cavour. In the midst of this motley clamor, one could hear on one side the loyalty of the authentic Catholics to Piux IX's fateful and solemn *"Non possumus"*; on the other, the helpless, angry cry of the antipapists. They unanimously demanded reforms, or rather, the radical and final suppression of the temporal power of the popes. With Pius IX, they shouted, the temporal power had perpetrated the most despotic and barbaric act ever seen by mankind. He had taken an innocent child away from his parents, abandoning them to the deepest sorrow and plunging an unhappy family forever into the most pathetic poverty.

Even some faithful Catholics remained disturbed and perplexed, not knowing which side to take. They often opted for a painful neutrality and a rather timid silence, an anticipated triumph for the enemies of the Church.

Everywhere, people of all kinds and opinions, from staunch believers to the most progressive, were asking several questions. "Do you know what happened? Pius IX took a child away from his parents. What do you think? Is it possible? How? And why?" These questions were followed by a discussion that highlighted all the malice of the "sons of the world" compared with the deplorable ignorance and guilelessness of the "sons of light". To the sacrilegious slanders and hypocritical protests of the rebels,

the good ones could often respond only with bland astonishment and guilty silence.

We repeat, however, that the battle was waged mainly
in France. From every perspective, during that era, France
was the point toward which everything converged. In
commerce, in industry, above all in military strategy,
France was always on the front line, led by the nephew
of the first Bonaparte. Napoleon III was an extraordinarily gifted man, born and trained to dominate others and
take them to where he wanted. Great Caesar, *Empereur
par excellence*, he was unfortunately duped by the Masonic
sects, which he passively obeyed.

While in command as the arbiter of the destiny of all
nations, determining with supreme power who should
govern them, he ostensibly protected the Pope with troops
he kept in Rome. In reality, in a subtle, hidden way, he
was helping the subalpine king to achieve the unity of Italy,
founded on the ruins of the other thrones. Slowly, public opinion was being prepared to accept the sacrilegious
conclusion of the deplorable campaign to dethrone the
Pope. All this was done under the pretext of protecting
and promoting *freedom* and *independence*, to restore order
in the Papal States. But it was an order disturbed by Napoleon himself, along with Vittorio Emanuele, through the
Masonic clubs. In short, Napoleon III was the nineteenth
century's Pilate, who handed the Christ of God over to the
executioner, washing his own hands, as the great Bishop of
Poitiers, Monseigneur Louis Pie, rightly pointed out. Being
the man of "ten consciences", as the great Don Giacomo
Margotti put it, in his column in *L'Armonia*, the Catholic
daily newspaper of Turin, the emperor wanted to find a
definitive solution to the case of the Mortara child.

So, Napoleon III, far from siding with Pius IX and the
Church that he pretended to protect, far from imposing

silence on the desecrating attacks of the wicked, at least until the matter was clarified, disapproved a priori of the Pope's conduct, revealing his "inner resentment" to one of his generals, Monsieur de la Tour, in the following terms: "What? While I protect the Pope with my troops, he in return commits these blunders? This annoys me greatly."

Behold the new Pilate, who treats the Pope like a child, or the new Herod Antipas, who mocks him as an incompetent.

This attitude of the great Caesar of the modern age could not help but favor the enemies of the Church and the papacy. They, with all the fury of which they were capable, railed against the great Pius IX. They spewed their vengeance and their gall in bitter diatribes, atrocious invectives, and sacrilegious calumnies, echoed from the rostrums, the casinos, the cafés, and especially from the theaters and the press. Everywhere there was talk about nothing but the Mortara child, sacrificed, as they said, to the tyrannical whims of Pius IX, imprisoned, tortured, martyred with great satisfaction by that barbarian, who laughed and enjoyed hearing the sighs and groans of the disconsolate parents.

Of course, the fact lent itself to melodramatic emotions. This is why the theater seized upon "poor little Mortara". A play or operetta entitled *The Fortune-Teller* was produced and caused a sensation. The audience watched a child clinging to the white robe of Pius IX, trying to stop him as the latter snatched him from his mother's arms. This operetta, staged in Paris, reflected exactly the opinion that was forming around this now famous subject. Noblewomen shed tears while watching it. In the hands of the revolutionaries and the wicked, the play turned into the basis of the satanic fury that periodicals and magazines of the times flung at the face of the august Pontiff.

In that situation appeared the great Louis Veuillot, chief editor of *L'Univers*, which he founded and directed: there he was, going down to the arena, despite the tremendous threats of the furious, almighty Caesar. Veuillot, this intrepid leader, this avant-garde sentinel, this fearless hero, waved the Catholic flag, clear and pure, intact and immaculate. He was alone in the large crowd of sophists, lawyers, judges, aristocrats, diplomats, government leaders, ministers, princes, and kings who were conspiring and shouting against the Christ of God. The magnanimous Veuillot was the very personification of Catholic stoicism. He lifted his voice in defense of Pius IX, reflecting and synthesizing in his laudable articles the opinion of the Catholic world, which had yielded the floor to him. He refuted objections, clarified doubts, and affirmed the rights of the Church; he suffered with serenity and admirable resignation the ridicule and the atrocious calumnies of the rebels. Veuillot summed up in one word the entire course of this stormy dispute, in order to show the whole world the triumphant Catholic flag. He treated the Mortara case in such a way that the prestige of those who disagreed would turn into disgust, and indeed, anyone who dared to bring up those slanders again was ridiculed.

It was a magnificent triumph that brought the matter back to the point of departure, putting things in their right place and offering tremendous support to the Roman Question, which the Mortara case was dragging toward a tragic solution.

In short, the great Veuillot won not only a return match but also the undisputed victory. He who writes these lines cannot help but place on the cold tomb that encloses the mortal remains of the great polemicist, the valiant coryphaeus of Catholic journalism, the testimony of the most heartfelt agreement, the sincerest and deepest gratitude.

Having reached this stage of the famous matter, let us look now at the angelic, admirable, immortal Pontiff. He was inside this thick, dark cloud, inside this confused vortex of disputes and controversy. He was far above the frothing, angry waves of the human passions that conspired with Hell to wage a war without quarter against the Church of Christ. Pius IX did not let himself be intimidated by the lightning bolts of the fury of the mighty or by the thunder of Caesar's anger. Like a new Moses, he remained on the slopes of Sinai, still wrapped in the thick fog of the majesty of that great God who was his strength in combat. He beheld the distressing sight of an apostate humanity gone astray and suffered with sublime resignation. Imitating the divine heroism of the Man of Sorrows, the crucified God, Pius IX gave no other response to the protests, the insults, and the desecrating attacks of the wicked, nor did he wield any other weapon in defense against their sacrilegious attacks than his sublime "*Non possumus.*" He was as great as his magnanimous heart, as fearless and invincible as the Lion of Judah.

Yes, Pius IX was truly great in his long, stormy pontificate. He was great and sublime in his generous and noble intransigence with the mutinous revolutionary crowds in 1848. He was great in his exile in Gaeta. He was great and sublime in proclaiming the glories of the Immaculate. He was great and sublime in publishing the *Syllabus*, that magnificent, immortal record of his opposition to the spirit of the modern era. He was especially great in confronting the Pilates and Herods who insulted him, calling for him to come down from his throne and renounce his kingship so as to adapt to the demands of contemporary civilization.

It is a fact, though, that true merit is found not in exalting oneself but in humbling oneself. The imitation of Jesus is evident especially in inclining toward the small and humble. Here then is the Pope who, in the midst of serious matters of great importance, with his mind full of generous, anxious solicitude for the government of all the churches, postpones everything, forgets everything, so as to deal with the future of a poor boy, whom a young maidservant made a son of God, a brother of Christ, an heir to eternal glory, in the bosom of a Jewish family. To save the soul of this child, the great Pontiff bears everything, makes himself liable to everything, sacrifices everything, risks even his own state in the presence of the fury and infernal tenacity of the enemies of God. For this same reason, Pius IX sees his dignity as Vicar of Christ dragged through the mud of the theaters and of the press of the freethinkers. Like his divine model, he became the object of derision, mockery, jokes, and cruel sarcasm by the populace, by the servants of the worst apostates and of renegade emperors. These humiliations place Pius IX at heights that no other great man of the earth could or will ever achieve, alongside Him who loved children so much, calling them the "greatest" in the Kingdom of Heaven, threatening with the lightning bolts of His divine wrath those who tried to harm them even in the slightest!

May the immortal Pontiff receive the homage of filial and eternal gratitude offered by his humble, unworthy protégé, mixed with the tears that flow from his deeply moved heart. May it be like a well-deserved crown on the tomb that encloses his glorious remains, which unbridled wickedness tried to desecrate by attacking the procession that was taking them to the Church of San Lorenzo al Verano. Good Catholics hope to see them raised to the honor of the altars and kissed with the deepest respect. In addition to the tribute of well-deserved praise that mankind and history will pay to the Pontiff of the Immaculate, to the *Syllabus*, and to the Vatican Council, may these words be engraved in gold letters that centuries will not efface, more eloquent than the most eloquent eulogy: "The Pontiff of the children".

After having given expression to sentiments of the most legitimate and sacred gratitude, let us return to the facts, noting the two salient points of the controversy that godlessness placed under the light of its torches in order to slander the dignity of the pontificate.

First point: Pius IX takes a child away from his parents.

Second point: this child discovers that he is baptized and Catholic, in spite of his parents and himself.

These are the crucial points of this huge, dreadful controversy.

We answered the first calumny above, reporting exactly the facts, of which our benevolent readers will make good use. Now let us refute the second calumny (the child finds out that he is Catholic *in spite of himself*: since we concede that he was and is, against the will of his parents and family), drawing attention to a fact that we will point out in the following pages.

The supernatural instinct of grace in young Mortara

By "supernatural instinct" we mean the practical, instinctive conviction with reference to the supernatural order and the actions that derive from it. All this is the result of a form of knowledge prior to any investigation and reflection by reason and consciousness.

Baptism, as sacred theology teaches, is the supernatural regeneration of the soul that leaves on it, as an indelible mark, a similarity and a real relationship between the regenerated soul and its divine model. This regeneration, or supernatural rebirth, is like a second essence or nature, superimposed on and grafted onto the first, original nature, as Saint Paul proclaimed. Hence, this new essence or nature must have its own instinct, with its corresponding movements and acts. This divine economy of grace was manifested in the Mortara child, and we will briefly show its features.

But first we must point out that the education he received from his parents was Jewish in the broadest sense and also in the stricter, more rigorous connotation of the word. In the time that we write about (1851–1858), the ideas of deplorable eclecticism and fatal tolerance in religious matters, which cause so much destruction nowadays, had not yet appeared in society.

Freedom of worship and of thought was indeed an error professed by writers and schools, but it did not enjoy the official status that it has now, nor had it received any institutional or legal sanction.

Moreover, between the Talmud and the Gospels, the synagogue and the Catholic Church, Jews and Christians, there was an abyss, a traditional antipathy, a very bitter antagonism. It was like the Great Wall of China, an insurmountable barrier that separated one group from the other, hindering any interaction, any compromise, any mingling and confusion. To use an exact and apt expression: it prevented any crossbreeding.

The Edgardo boy had never heard of Christ, or the Church, or the Pope, or Christians, who never set foot in his house. They would not even pass by the modest clothing store that was the commercial enterprise that provided an income for his parents and family. The little boy barely knew that there were Christians, who were never discussed at home, in either a good or a bad way.

Moreover, Edgardo, from his earliest childhood, had learned from his mother, a woman very devout in her beliefs, the first rudiments of the Mosaic religion. He prayed with her every day, reciting the customary prayers in Hebrew.

In the Jewish school that Edgardo attended when he was very young, he had been introduced to the history of the Mosaic faith and of the Talmud, and to the language of Palestine. He made progress in Hebrew, so much so that, when he was no more than four years old, he was able to read in public and official sessions of the Jewish community in Bologna. He received for his precocious zeal many gifts, candies, and toys.

From all this previous training, it is clear that the soul of the child felt, if not repulsion and hatred toward Christianity, at least very intense adherence to his parents' religion, compared with which Jesus, the Church, and Christians were foreign realities. What obviously emerged and was manifested at the bottom of his heart was a very exalted idea of God, accompanied by a feeling of deep respect and excessive fear. This fear was the natural result of the Law that had been proclaimed amid dense, dark clouds, amid the lightning and the deafening thunder of Mount Sinai. This Law, however, is also the point of transition and contact with another Law sanctioned among the peaceful, charming splendors of Mount Tabor by the transfigured Jesus, who inaugurated and set it forever in His loving, divine Heart, as a law of grace and love, as the real code of charity, mercy, clemency, and forgiveness for everyone.

Despite all this previous Mosaic training, and contrary to it, the Mortara child showed that he had a soul that was, as Tertullian puts it, *naturaliter christiana*: in short, having received Baptism (although he did not know it), he was a Christian by the supernatural instinct of grace.

At times, going out for a walk with the servant girl who had secretly baptized him, that blessed creature he could regard as his mother in Christ, and seeing that, passing in front of a church, Anna made the Sign of the Cross, Edgardo respectfully took his little hat off. If Anna entered one of those churches, the child followed her happily, so much so that sometimes he was the one to ask her to go inside, even though the young woman, fearing that the child's parents might learn about it, thought it prudent and proper not to grant this wish.

Edgardo still remembers with pleasure that, while with his mother one day on a square in Bologna, at the moment when the solemn procession of San Petronio, patron of the city, was passing by, he manifested a keen and impatient desire to watch that Christian procession. So as not to disappoint him, his mother agreed, even though she then quickly and hurriedly pulled him away by the hand, prompted by some inner qualms. For his part, Edgardo tried to hold back his mother; a childish struggle that had no other explanation but what is called, and I do call, the "supernatural sense of grace".

It is not strange that the devil, who according to the teaching of Saint Thomas "judges the inner dispositions of grace from the external acts", deducing from the aforementioned facts that the child belonged to Christ (who would soon claim him for Himself), relentlessly manifested more than once his anger and hatred.

We will report two events that more clearly highlight the supernatural work of grace in the little neophyte.

One day Edgardo was ill in the house of one of his uncles. On the threshold of his room he saw a huge dog with a horribly evil, satanic look. The child screamed in fear, indeed with the utmost terror, so that those who were in the house rushed to his room immediately. Made aware of what had happened, they started to look for but could not find the frightening mastiff. The memory of the dog still haunts Edgardo, and for him it is unforgettable.

Another time, shortly before the orders that led to his separation from his family were carried out, Edgardo needed to step out of his room to go to another part of the house. He heard, but did not recall how or from where, a cry that was not at all human—a cry so distressing, gloomy, and terrifying, revealing a fit of rage and diabolic wrath, that the child was frightened. He began to scream for help and quickly jumped into the arms of his mother, who was in the house. She had come running together with other members of the family and asked the child questions, to which he replied through his tears and sobs.

We relate these episodes without evaluating them, refraining from any comment about their possible preter-natural character. Now let us record other facts of much greater importance.

How to explain, if not by the influence of this same supernatural spirit, the constant and firm imperturbability of the child? In the most searing moment of the tragic and sorrowful separation from his parents, he did not complain or cry or put up the least resistance. Although he shed tears and called for his mother after he was taken from the house, just a few kind words were enough to calm him down completely. He did not cry anymore or ask about his family.

How to explain such docility and goodwill in a seven-year-old boy who had been raised very carefully in the Mosaic religion, which is completely antithetical to the Catholic religion? He gladly agrees to receive, from the two ladies traveling with him to Rome, the rudiments of the Faith. With pleasure he learns the basic Christian prayers, the Our Father and the Hail Mary. For the first time the sweet names of Jesus and Mary penetrate his young heart. He receives with joy the Brown Scapular, which from then on he never abandoned. Thus he continues to experience the supernatural motherhood, which, for the first time, manifested itself in the soul of that providential girl who regenerated his soul with the Sacrament of Baptism.

Since those fortunate moments, Edgardo has been a Christian. It is as though he had been born that way. He belongs, with all the strength of his soul, to the motherly bosom of the Church, his adoptive Mother. He wants to visit Catholic churches, to pray with the Church. He already begins to pray for his parents, for whom he would always preserve a very filial, very tender affection.

But there is more. This same power of the grace that was working so effectively in Edgardo's soul had to become evident and to triumph in circumstances that were rather critical and dangerous for his still young faith.

Here he is, facing his father and his grieving mother, who had both arrived, determined to go back to Bologna with Edgardo. His father breaks out into shouts and threats; his mother succumbs to her overwhelming sorrow in front of the imperturbable child. He does not lament or shed a tear. He does not show the slightest desire to return with his disconsolate parents, if only to relieve their deep sorrow. On the contrary, he shudders and trembles, running to Don Enrico Sarra, the rector, seeking protection.

There is even more. For a whole month, or maybe two, the child's parents will visit him every day at the house of the same rector. They insist, they beg him, they implore him to return to the family to embrace his afflicted siblings, who are inconsolable because they see him no more. His mother, his poor, humiliated mother, speaks more with sobs and abundant tears than with words, and she hugs and presses him to her broken heart. They both make him a thousand promises that should suffice to win over a child and overcome his perseverance. They promise him many gifts and a gold watch. In short, they use all the expedients, wiles, and stratagems that nature may suggest in similar circumstances, found with that dexterity that only a father and a loving mother have to penetrate the heart of their beloved son. Nevertheless, the child remains unyielding, imperturbable, and in fact indifferent to this subtle and truly formidable strategy of nature. In rejecting the irresistible attempts of motherly love, the tears, sighs, and sobs of a mother, he is protected by the invulnerable shield of grace. He wields only one weapon; he formulates only one protest; he responds with only one word, that of the Apostles, confessors, and early martyrs: "I am a Christian, if you want me to come with you, there is only one way: be converted too."

One day, the young neophyte spoke to his mother with great conviction, mixed with filial affection and tenderness, about the sublime mysteries of the Catholic religion, about the most Blessed Virgin Mary, the Holy Scapular. The mother, moved and softened, burst into tears and said: "I too, I too want this Scapular of the Madonna."

As soon as his father realized what was happening, he took his wife by an arm and abruptly separated her from the child.

My afflicted and beloved mother! Who would not be moved by seeing your tears and deep sorrow? In these tragic events, you have no other role than that of the most loving mother, the mother overwhelmed by sorrow. Will there be no one, then, to have pity and compassion on you, along with your fortunate son? Your beloved son weeps with you, deeply moved. He understands your inconsolable sorrow, your abundant tears. He deplores the fact that a hapless hand frustrated the movement of grace that, in that solemn moment, through the Immaculate Heart of Mary, penetrated your tormented breast to dress your wounds by contact with the Heart of Christ, which was wounded by love for us. Her sorrow was inconsolable, and it will be again, if her soul is not open to the joyful, sweet hope that a day will come when the two loving hearts of mother and child will meet again forever united in the divine, adorable Heart of the Divine Redeemer, amid the celestial splendors of eternal happiness!

Since that memorable day when the light of divine grace shone in the disconsolate soul of the simple, innocent, but eloquent word of a child, his parents no longer showed up. Edgardo was not to see them again until many years later.

Hell succumbed, in the battle fought in the tender heart of that seven-year-old child between natural love and affection and the power of grace. The result for the child was complete and absolute detachment from his parents and family and a strong, lasting adherence to the maternal bosom of the Catholic Church, which had adopted him through the great Pope Pius IX. The latter, with the utmost dread, investigated the possibility of an attempt to kidnap the child or to abduct him violently.

When young Edgardo was in public, in large crowds, the Pope always showed great uneasiness, fearing that "they could steal him", as he put it simply. This caused frequent jokes among Edgardo's fellow students and companions, who sometimes laughed at the naïve innocence of the child, who was afraid of being "stolen" as if he were "a precious object" (as they used to say in amusement).

The feeling of fear and embarrassment was evident in Edgardo, especially in the very frequent situations in which foreigners from every nation, drawn by curiosity, wanted to see "little Mortara", and in particular when the class of the college to which he belonged walked through the ghetto, or the Jewish district.

In short, the young neophyte was so far from wanting to return to his family that, with a feeling of deep horror, he used to shiver at the most distant prospect of such a possibility.

Let modern naturalism now try to explain satisfactorily the phenomena of grace just mentioned. Let it explain how, despite the most punctilious Jewish education, such an extraordinary metamorphosis came about in that young life. Let it stop, therefore, being an accomplice of godlessness and of the Masonic sects that repeat ad nauseam that Pius IX had committed the most horrendous outrages, trampling the sacred rights of nature in order to snatch a child from his parents and forcing him "unwillingly" to renounce the synagogue in order to profess Catholicism "in a compulsory, unconscious manner"!

To the ignoble slander repeated so many times by the unbelieving press, that Edgardo remained locked in a sort of prison by order of Pius IX and was exposed to the most barbaric treatment, we will reply later. We will do justice by relating the facts exactly. Let us turn now to the child's family, pointing out his contacts with them.

The Mortara child and his relationship with his parents and his family

The admirable inner movement of grace that was acting in the young neophyte, which we called "supernatural instinct", was not opposed nevertheless to his legitimate feelings of filial love. On the contrary, it gave them a solid foundation and strong support. Given that real love consists in desiring true good for the beloved person, Edgardo began right away to pray for his parents and his siblings. He asked God, through the powerful intercession of the Immaculate Virgin (whom he loved as his own Mother), to deliver them from "darkness and the shadow of death", by removing the veil in their hearts that hid the truth and leading them gently into the Kingdom of His Son, to enjoy the admirable light preserved by the Church, His Holy Bride. He prayed this so that they too might know the one God and His Messenger, Jesus Christ our Lord. This was the wish and the pure desire that young Mortara offered to God from the very beginning of his faith, trusting the infinite Mercy of the Redeemer and the fervent prayers of those who cared about his situation and joined their intentions to his and their prayers to the child's innocent supplication.

Some time had passed since the last meeting of the son with his parents, who had returned to their house in Bologna. The main concern of the directors of the college at Saint Peter in Chains and Edgardo's keen desire was to give evidence to the family of his filial affection. Edgardo wanted to take this opportunity to express the joy that he was experiencing in the bosom of his adoptive Mother, the Catholic Church, as well as the lively impatience with which he was waiting for the happy day when he could see his beloved parents and siblings embrace the true religion and recognize and confess Christ as the Son of God.

Of course, his still very tender age did not allow his letters to be exclusively his work. The supervisors intervened, faithfully and accurately interpreting the desires of the young boarding school student. Since the family could not help but realize this fact, they considered these letters as not being from Edgardo, equating form and content, and they disregarded them without replying.

Edgardo did not let this discourage him. He continued to write to his parents through his directors, taking the pen in hand himself as soon as he could. He insisted on reiterating his filial affection, but even more on expressing his deep satisfaction in possessing the truth. He wished that his family might possess it as the greatest good and the most enviable happiness. He added that, as soon as his beloved parents and siblings embraced the authentic religion, there would no longer be any obstacle to his rejoining them to enjoy their company, once his education was finished.

Despite the fact that these letters were written by Edgardo himself, they never received any reply, because his family was steadfast in their belief that the letters' composition was the work of his directors.

For this reason the letters became less frequent. Edgardo limited himself to expressing occasionally to his beloved parents and relatives the same constant feelings of deep respect and filial affection that animated him. At the same time, he pointed out to them the deep sadness caused him by the fact that his letters remained unanswered, and the hope he cherished that finally they would respond and send him news about them, news that he very impatiently desired to receive.

All these expressions of the affection, desires, and hopes of young Edgardo remained completely frustrated. Now he no longer counted on receiving any reply from his family, and he had decided to suspend such an unproductive correspondence when, on May 7, 1867, in the month of Mary, while he was already a novice in the Order of the Canons Regular of the Lateran, he received an unexpected letter from his father. This letter began with the following words:

My dearest Edgardo,

Certainly you will not have thought that your parents and family have forgotten about you. The reason we did not write to you until now was that the only thing that was yours in your letters was the name, while all the rest was the work of other hands.

But now that you have reached a certain age and maturity, we can write to each other without the mediation of any kind of censorship.

It is not possible to describe the deep satisfaction that Edgardo felt in receiving the abovementioned letter, to which he hurried to reply as thoroughly as possible and with all the outpouring of tender, filial affection. Thus began a monthly and often bimonthly correspondence between him and his family, which was to last for three years. The domestic and family relations were reestablished completely, and the young man took advantage of any opportunity, particularly of the illness or death of a relative, to show loyalty and filial respect to his parents and his family. He used all the terms and expressions of affection and preferred to overstep the limits or to exaggerate rather than to limit himself to a concise or dry style that might lead to misinterpretations. In this way he gave more than one proof of the truthfulness and sincerity of his feelings.

One of these proofs was when, after repeated requests, he sent them his portrait (a rare exception to the rule, granted by the superiors, given the family's circumstances), requesting also a visit to his parents by those confreres who were moving from Rome to Florence or Turin. He received with great pleasure the visit of his uncle Signor Moscato, who traveled to meet and embrace Edgardo on behalf of his parents and siblings. In short, he left no room for the slightest doubt about the affection that every good son must profess for his parents. In this way, he provided in advance the necessary facts to refute the slanders later invented by the enemies of the papacy who were eager for revenge.

The correspondence to which we refer had, for the moment, a retrospective effect that we hasten to point out.

As we mentioned above, we will return to report the facts on this point accurately.

Edgardo had entered the Order of the Canons of the Holy Redeemer at the Lateran and, as of November 17, 1867, had made his simple profession, at the age of only sixteen, accompanied by the special blessings of Pope Pius IX. The Pope approved his decision and confirmed it, allowing the young man (in keeping with his wish) to change his name from Edgardo to Pio Maria, while he kept repeating with satisfaction: "Good for Father Pio Maria Mortara! Good for Father Pio Maria Mortara!"

The parents, however, were completely unaware of what had happened. In view of the recent legislation, very favorable to parental rights but detrimental to personal freedom and divine law, it was imperative to obtain the father's retrospective consent to confirm and sanction the decision Edgardo had made to dedicate himself entirely to God.

Opposed to this, however, was the sine qua non condition stipulated from the beginning of the family correspondence, that "we must never talk about any matter regarding religion."

It was therefore necessary first to obtain permission to address the subject. Edgardo asked his father for it. He agreed, after learning correctly that it was not about discussing religion, but only about confiding a secret. The young man told his parents the news about the kind and nature of the state that he had just entered. He added, in clear terms for them, who knew nothing about Catholicism, that he had embraced a "religious state", the same taken by those who honestly get married. He said that, in this decision, he had obeyed a deliberate and free movement of his will, without the interference of any kind of pressure or coercion. He related that, although on the basis of this free choice he had renounced all material possessions, consecrating himself entirely to God, this did not prevent him, as a good son, from loving with all his soul his dear parents and family, and taking an interest in their true happiness.

To all this, his parents replied that "if that was his decision, and if he had made it freely, they had no objection, and were completely satisfied."

Our readers should pay close attention to the words just cited, to which we will have to refer again soon.

In all their letters, the parents did not withhold deserved praise for the superiors (whom they always called "Very reverend sirs") of the young professed religious, for the care that these religious individuals had for his welfare and education. His father and mother testified in this way to their deep gratitude and repeated the same praises to the Canons who, while traveling to Florence (where the Mortaras had moved from Turin, after having left Bologna), paid them a visit, on behalf of Edgardo, delivering his letters. All this appeared to be implicit approval of the decision made by their son about his religious vocation, which had already been revealed to the parents.

From the first letters exchanged between them and their son, their strong desire to see their beloved boy was clear; at first they insisted that he himself pay them a visit in Florence, where they were residing at the time to which we refer (1867–1869). They soon ceased, however, given the warnings of the young professed religious, whose Holy Rule and other very substantial reasons of prudence and reserve did not allow him to leave the Papal States to travel to the capital of the alleged Kingdom of Italy, where ruled a usurper king, the sworn enemy of the papacy and the Roman Church.

The sanctity of the religious state that he had just embraced and the sacred rights of freedom of conscience so highly praised and celebrated by the *Italianissimi*, as they used to call the conspirators and the agitators for the cause of unity against everything and everybody, stood between him and his family, as a barrier that was insurmountable from every point of view.

To the abovementioned warnings by the professed religious, which were limited to citing the rule that allowed no visits by the religious to their families, except in cases of extreme urgency, the Mortaras responded in the most correct forms of deference and respect to those requirements, announcing the possibility of a trip to Rome for the purpose of embracing their beloved Edgardo.

Despite repeated reassurances and announcements, however, they never set the date for this visit, which greatly perplexed Edgardo, who wanted nothing more than its immediate realization.

Meanwhile, the political events related to the Roman Question developed rapidly. All good Catholics, faithful in their heart to the Pope-King, already foresaw and sensed the sad, dismal conclusion, which would lead to the violent, tyrannical occupation of the mutilated remains of Saint Peter's Patrimony and in particular of Rome.

On September 2, 1870, the terrible defeat of the French troops by the Prussians at the Battle of Sedan coincided with the withdrawal of those troops from Rome, by express order of Napoleon III, the Caesar of Paris. It coincided also with the proclamation of the dogma of papal infallibility during the Vatican Council and with that council's unexpected suspension. All these events accumulated and amassed like furious waves on the stormy sea of political struggles. It was like the roar of thunder announcing the rapidly approaching storm.

Countless hesitations and vacillations followed, threats, satanic deceptions, and evil machinations by the enemies of the Pope's temporal power, led by the wretched

parvenu king Vittorio Emanuele, who would soon be prey
to desperate remorse. On September 20, 1870, the can-
nons of the sacrilegious king and princes conspiring against
the Vicar of Christ echoed eerily and ominously from five
in the morning, drowning out the peaceful, gentle tolling
of the bell that invited the sons of the cloister to pray together for those who do not know God or who deliber-
ately deny Him and sin: "pro his qui ignorant et errant"
(on behalf of those who are ignorant and going astray).

Until ten in the morning, the terrible roar of the can-
nons did not diminish, and Edgardo, in union with his
brothers in religion, the Canons Regular of the Roman
monastery of Saint Peter in Chains, went into the temple
of the Lord to beg His Divine Majesty to deign to put an
end to the relentless battle, and not to allow "those who
ignore His Holy Name to devastate His sacred heritage".

At ten o'clock on the dot, the white flag of the Pontiff
waved over the dome of Saint Peter's, and he, like the
Lamb of God, was about to be delivered into the clutches
of the attacking wolves. His magnanimous, benevolent
heart could no longer allow the brave heroes who were
defending him to shed their blood and die for him. The
flag waving atop the Vatican put an end to the fighting.
But that does not mean that the Pope yielded to the principle of "might makes right" and to the brutal theory of
"fait accompli". Among its white folds, the flag did give
a glimpse of the terrible lightning of the Divine Justice,
which showed the Italian Belshazzar the day and time of
tremendous and inescapable reprisals.

With the signing of the armistice, soldiers penetrated
through the open breach of Porta Pia, thereafter dese-
crated with the dismal name of "Gate of September 20".

We will not pause to record the deplorable historical
events—it would be better to call them ignoble, shameful

orgies—that occurred in three days of complete anarchy caused by the entry of the Piedmont forces into the Eternal City. Rome became another Jerusalem, delivered over to the fury and satanic rage of the enemies of the papacy. Contemporary history will brand these sad acts with fiery letters, condemning the wicked invaders, but we will not speak about them, because they are not part of the outline that we proposed to follow. We will report only, as relevant to our story, that among the fierce screams emitted by the sectarians and revolutionaries who like a swarm of beasts invaded the city of the popes, one stood out as an echo of the godlessness that demanded revenge. "The Mortara child! Let us go to Saint Peter in Chains!" shouted the possessed Masons. "Let us go and carry off the Mortara child, so as to return him to his unhappy parents!" Certainly, only an act of special Providence kept the mutinous crowd from carrying out its sacrilegious plan.

Good Pius IX, at the sight of the many crimes committed in those baleful days, suffered from a sorrow equal to, if not surpassing, the greatness and magnanimity of his soul. In the midst of such horrible trials and many worries that accumulated in his tormented heart, he did not forget (who would ever have thought it?) poor Edgardo. The great Pontiff of the *Syllabus*, of the Immaculate, and of the Vatican Council, as is true only of a really great man, cared even about the smallest things: "et exaltavit humiles" (and He has exalted the lowly), as it says in the Magnificat of the Blessed Virgin Mary. The great Pius IX was still the "Pontiff of the Mortara child". While in the company of his domestic prelates and the cardinals who went to console him, he would anxiously ask: "Has Edgardo not left Rome yet?"

Indeed, since the day of the occupation, the venerable superiors of the young man, fearful that some sad incident could happen to him, had thought of getting him out of Rome and Italy and sending him abroad. The Most Reverend Father Passeri, General of the Order, had consulted His Eminence Giacomo Cardinal Antonelli, His Holiness' Secretary of State, about this question. The Cardinal, however, did not think such a decision should be made, as the matter did not yet seem urgent. It may have seemed to him more appropriate for the young professed not to try to flee, as the usurper government would have made it impossible and then would have taken severe reprisals against it. His opinion was this: "Wait and protect against possible risks or dangers." Events, however, rushed headlong.

In mid-October 1870, Salomone Levi Mortara appeared at the monastery of Saint Peter in Chains, accompanied by his son Arnoldo. He expressed the desire to visit his son Edgardo. The joy that this sudden, unexpected visit caused the young man was inseparable from a certain anxiety and sad foreboding, which his superiors shared with him.

Edgardo met his father accompanied by the Reverend Father Luigi Santini, master of the professed religious, under whose direction they were being educated and formed in the religious spirit. His father welcomed him with obvious affection but with some reserve that the son could not help but notice. Moreover, Arnoldo forgot to give him a fraternal embrace, which he gave only after an explicit request by their father.

After a long conversation, in which, of course, family news and expressions of mutual affection were exchanged, father and son parted on the most affectionate terms. Signor Mortara repeated to his son the invitation to come to the hotel where he was staying and to spend the day with him, have lunch with the family, and enjoy together the reciprocal relations of paternal and filial affection, provided that he could get the required permission from his superiors. They, however, were not at all likely to grant permission, foreseeing the dangerous consequences of a visit at the hotel in such critical political circumstances, among foreigners and perhaps hostile, ill-intentioned people. Edgardo, therefore, hastened to write his father a very polite letter, begging him to take no offense if, for easily understandable prudential reasons, he could not meet to return the visit.

A few days later Signor Mortara arrived again, accompanied by Arnoldo. After spending a while with him, he told him of his decision to leave Rome and return to Florence.

The young man was very surprised, because in their first meeting his father had told him of his plan to extend his stay in Rome. Since he had gathered, with the permission of his superiors, some small gifts for his beloved mother and his dear family, he hastened to hand them over to his father, at the same time commending to him his most cordial, affectionate greetings for everybody.

When they embraced one last time, Edgardo had the charming, refined idea of giving him another very filial, affectionate hug for his beloved mother, adding with great simplicity: "I give this hug to you so that you can pass it on to my dear mother."

His father received the embrace with some hesitation and with a somewhat ambiguous smile, which at the moment surprised Edgardo but whose significance he would grasp a little later.

In fact, the following day, one of the Canons told him that he had seen his father taking a walk around the city. Some antipapal and republican magazines published the following notice in huge print: "The father of the Mortara child has arrived in this Capital to reclaim his son Edgardo, who was brutally taken away from him by the Pope. He hopes to get him back by appealing to the government of His Majesty Vittorio Emanuele."

For the child this news was like a bolt of lightning from a clear sky. The surprise and the horrible fear it caused him were rekindled every time he was reminded of it. As he instinctively recalled his father's very recent goodbye, his father's smile on the threshold of Saint Peter in Chains came to his mind like a frightening flash of lightning, only to sink then into his afflicted heart like the icy, piercing point of a dagger.

After he recovered from that initial sudden gasp, however, his first thought was to turn to prayer, trusting in Divine Providence and in the paternal vigilance of his superiors. He repeated from the depths of his soul: "In te Domine speravi! Non confundar in aeternum!" (In you, O LORD, I seek refuge; let me never be put to shame) (Ps 31:1). His pleas and prayers ascended to the throne of the Divine Majesty, which would crown the previous graces with the most illustrious grace, if one can say that: with the providential preservation of his religious vocation.

Confirmation and personal ratification of his Baptism

The best and most categorical answer to the inventions of the anti-Catholic periodicals, which presented the young man as "reluctantly" baptized and Catholic, kept prisoner in the college of Saint Peter in Chains, burdened—as they said—by the heavy, unbearable chains of popery and superstition, the most categorical denial of these shameful lies and slanders was what I call his "confirmation and personal ratification" of his Baptism and Confirmation by the magnanimous Pontiff of the Immaculate. As we related earlier, from the age of seven and for a long time, thanks to the visible intervention of Divine Providence, and by his own request, the Mortara child was entrusted by Pope Pius IX to the Canons Regular of the Lateran in Saint Peter in Chains. He remained in the college that they ran until he was thirteen, devoting himself to his studies of Latin, in the elementary school and then in the high school, under the direction of several fathers of the abovementioned Order.

At the age of eleven, in 1862, he had received for the first time the Eucharist, the Bread of Angels, from the hands of His Eminence Paul Cardinal Cullen, Archbishop of Dublin and Primate of Ireland. Ever since then, he became very fond of the way of life and the spirit of the institute and of the Congregation of Canons. He liked to pray and to chant the Divine Office with them. When he was thirteen, therefore, he begged the Most Reverend Father Abbot General Don Giovanni Strozzi, who was very well known in Italy and abroad for his virtues and erudition, to admit him to the abovementioned community as an aspirant. After the usual tests, on November 30, 1864, young Edgardo was entrusted to the Reverend Father Don Luigi Santini, director of the professed Canons of Saint Peter in Chains. He, with the greatest care and paternal affection, initiated the young aspirant to the spirit of the apostolic Order.

Since the certificate of his Baptism was not in any parish register, because of the well-known exceptional circumstances, and since he had, at the time, no contacts with his family, for the reasons we noted earlier, it was believed that he had already reached the age of fifteen. Upon examination of the civil records in Bologna, his birthplace, with the help of the Most Reverend Father Feletti, Inquisitor General at the time of the so-called abduction of the child, it turned out that Don Pio was born on August 27, 1851. Consequently, in 1865 he was only fourteen years old. Therefore, despite his intense desire, he had to resign himself to waiting another year.

The most important reason to embrace the religious state was, for Don Pio, the instinctive conviction that he could not help consecrating himself entirely to God's service, since he had been filled with so many and such distinguished favors and very special graces. This way, he could, though unworthily and imperfectly, return to the Divine Majesty what he had received from Him in such extraordinary ways. Of the many religious orders that were flourishing, he decided to enroll in the one that, through entirely providential circumstances and with the sacred approval of the Supreme Pontiff, had received the mission to catechize the child and to educate and direct him in piety and knowledge.

Finally, the much-desired hour arrived, and on October 7, 1866, the Reverend Father Santini, the director of the professed religious and General Visitor of the Order, entrusted the young postulant to the Reverend Father Don Alfonso Lalli, the master of novices. Under his direction, Don Pio prepared to take the holy habit, which he received on October 7, 1867, from the hands of the abovementioned Most Reverend Father Don Giovanni Strozzi, the Abbot General. The latter, as the solemn ceremony was being celebrated, recalled the very special graces that the infinite Mercy of God had dispensed to the fortunate postulant, and applied to him very appropriately the words of the prophet Isaiah: "I was ready to be sought by those who did not ask for me; I was ready to be found by those who did not seek me." He then exhorted him, as he consecrated himself to God, to strive to correspond to the grace that had predestined and chosen him, to the point of granting him a religious vocation. Indeed, as well stated by the great Pontiff Saint Gregory, the greater the graces received, the stricter and more severe will be the account of them that must be rendered.

Edgardo took the holy habit along with his classmate Antonio Calvino. The ceremony took place in the Constantinian Basilica of Saint Agnes Outside the Walls in Rome, in the church dedicated to that holy virgin and martyr who is loved so much by all who have read her admirable life, the brave girl, a prodigy of virtue and heroism, whose precious little statue—as mentioned above—Pius IX had given to Don Pio nine years earlier. Thus, the Pope had, as it were, foreseen the vocation of that child kneeling at his feet, placing him from then on under the patronage and care of the noble virgin, so that she might protect and defend him against the snares of Hell and the dangerous enticements of the devil and of the flesh.

There, in that house repaired by the Pontiff himself, next to the tomb of the saint, in thanksgiving for his miraculous preservation from the terrible misfortune of April 12, 1854, when the floor collapsed, Don Pio, under the paternal, intelligent direction of the Reverend Father Lalli, was being formed in the spirit of the Order of the Canons. After the twelve months of the novitiate, he prepared to take simple vows, when, on October 22, 1867, the unfortunate, dismal news of the march of Garibaldi's troops on the Eternal City spread like a thunderclap. Garibaldi himself was leading them, and they were heading for Rome right through the Via Nomentana.

All fathers and novices who were in the house of Saint Agnes, located on the same Via Nomentana (with the exception of Father Lalli), moved back to Saint Peter in Chains, where they remained in seclusion until the arrival of the French troops in Rome. Thanks to these troops, the ferocious invasion of Garibaldi's barbarians was repelled. The latter, trampling underfoot the most sacred international rights and employing the most abominable means, after committing atrocious crimes, set out to desecrate the sacred soil of the Eternal City. This they did in the name of the "Gentleman King" and of Italian culture, to regenerate and liberate Rome from the tyrannical rule of a ruthless Pope like Pius IX!

History will record in letters of fire the horrible crimes perpetrated by Garibaldi's troops, such as the indescribable attack on the Serristori barracks, in which many Zouaves died from an explosion caused by Giuseppe Monti and Gaetano Tognetti. History will also report in golden letters the heroic actions taken by brave Zouaves in Genzano and Montelibretti.

Due to these political events, Edgardo's profession of simple vows did not occur until November 17, 1867, in the Basilica of Saint Agnes Outside the Walls. The young man pronounced his simple vows together with the abovementioned Don Antonio Calvino and Giacomo Sciovalli, from Venice, with his hands in those of the Most Reverend Father Abbot Alberto Passari, then General of the Order and successor to the Most Reverend Giovanni Strozzi. The latter had died and was mourned in Rome, in Italy, and abroad by everyone, but especially by his disconsolate children, the Canons Regular of the Lateran and of Saint Augustine.

Edgardo will never forget the paternal, moving words that the abovementioned Most Reverend Father General addressed to him on that solemn occasion. He exhorted him to intensify his diligence and fervor in serving God, thus meriting new and greater graces, now that Divine Providence had reached the peak of its generosity, calling him to the mystical garden of religious life.

This way, he was enrolled in a very old and venerable Order. Its beginnings date back to the early Church, and its Holy Rule is the one the Apostles and their successors followed in the first Christian churches.

The great Father and Doctor of the Church Saint Augustine gave to his Canons in Hippo his spoken words and admirable example as their rule and constitution. Saint Gelasius, Saint Prospero, and Saint Possidius brought this rule, these constitutions, and their spirit to Rome, and they settled in the famous Basilica of the Lateran, the center of the Congregation and the mother and head of all churches in the world. From it came wise, illustrious, holy men who populated Europe and the world with new congregations of Canons Regular, which were fruitful in saints and scholars. Their number is sixteen thousand, and they have carried the light of faith and Catholic civilization to the most distant peoples.

On the same day, November 17, 1867, the young man returned to Saint Peter in Chains, where the Canons conducted their studies. He was received by Father Santini and admitted among the professed religious with his classmate Antonio Calvino.

Under the direction this wise, zealous teacher, Don Pio spent the years 1868 to 1870. At first he devoted himself to the study of literature and rhetoric, taught by Don Davide Farabulini, a priest from Ravenna and a former student of Pius Seminary, a distinguished man of letters and a poet. Later he studied the mathematical and philosophical sciences, in which he was guided by the same teacher of the professed religious, the abovementioned Father Santini, a lecturer and a doctor of philosophy and theology, who was highly respected and valued in the Order. Edgardo always looked to him as to his spiritual father, professing a very special esteem and appreciation. He then saw, with great satisfaction, that Father Santini was promoted to the high office of General Visitor and then General of the whole Order, after the death of the Most Reverend Father Passari.

These years of study passed without any unpleasant event overshadowing this peaceful, quiet stay, during which he was trained in literature and sciences and in the spirit of the apostolic sacred Order in which he had enrolled.

The great Pontiff who took charge of the Catholic education of the Jewish child approved and blessed his resolution to consecrate himself to God in that religious family. Besides granting him permission to take Pio as his religious name, he never failed to give him some bits of advice that were to constitute the program of his whole life.

When the young man appeared before His Holiness after taking simple vows, he prostrated himself at his feet with the humblest, most respectful attitude possible. "Do not forget, my son," Pius IX told him, "what Saint Francis de Sales teaches: that religious communities are similar to hospitals, where, in addition to the sick, there are also those who are convalescing, people recovering from a disease, and people who are cured. Which category do you belong to, my son? Is it not true, what I have just said?"

The most respectful silence was the answer.

But Pius IX did not limit himself to words, knowing very well that humility is the queen of all virtues and the most solid foundation for religious perfection. He wanted Don Pio to be formed in this virtue from the earliest stages of the religious life that he had embraced, not only from a theoretical point of view, but also on a practical level.

Allow us to mention the following event, in which shone the eminent wisdom and the incomparable paternal benevolence with which the immortal Pontiff honored his protégé.

It was the eve of the feast of the great Doctor and Pope Saint Gregory. The young professed religious at Saint Peter in Chains (one of whom was Edgardo), supervised by Father Santini, lined up two by two, put on their white

woolen habit and the *rocchetto* (surplice), which was partially covered and hidden under a foot-length black cloak,
gathered modestly in the front. They were heading for the
basilica of the Holy Father *in monte Coelio* (on the Caelian
Hill). After a short time, during which they had knelt to
worship the Divine Majesty in the tabernacle, they heard
the joyful ringing of the bells announcing the arrival of
Pius IX, accompanied by his court. The young Canons
immediately went to the main door of the basilica to kiss
the holy foot of His Holiness.

When Pius IX passed in front of Edgardo, the latter, in a
sudden burst of deep veneration and filial love, which was
quite understandable in the one who had been the "Mortara child", and even more so on such an occasion, rushed
to plant the most affectionate kiss on the foot of the one to
whom, after God, he owed everything. Unfortunately,
instead of reaching the foot, he collided with His Holiness'
knee, with such force that he received from it a strong
blow to the forehead. Pius IX would have fallen backward
if one of the domestic prelates, acting promptly, had not
supported him. After sizing up the whole situation, Pius
IX said nothing and kept walking forward.

All eyes were fixed on the young man, vacillating from
an expression of terror to another of tacit but bitter rebuke
for his energetic and legitimate yet clumsy rush of filial
affection.

Poor Edgardo, utterly ashamed, trembling, his face fiery
red, did not dare to raise his eyes. He followed His Holiness with his fellow students and the procession. All his
frightened limbs were shaken by an unstoppable shivering.
He answered with silence and secret repentance the solic-
itous, anxious question everybody seemed to be asking
him: "What have you done? You almost caused Pius IX
to fall, perhaps endangering his precious life—unwittingly,
of course!"

It was a question that, like a thunderclap, resounded in the ears of the repentant, disconsolate young man.

Truly similar to the good Cyrenian or to the faithful women who accompanied the Lord to the slopes of Calvary, he followed the others until they all arrived at that sacred place called the Triclinium, where Saint Gregory used to give a daily meal to twelve poor men, among whom he merited one day to welcome and assist the King of the poor, Jesus Himself.

Pius IX visited that place of devotion, paying attention to everything with the liveliest interest. When he was about to leave, he turned to Edgardo and, in a tone that was seemingly stern but in reality kindly (as was always the case with the angelic Pope, even in spite of himself), he said: "Come here. Kneel down before me."

The whole court and the swelling crowd fixed their eyes on the unfortunate young man, who, trembling and pale as a man mounting the gallows, obeyed immediately and prostrated himself at the Pontiff's feet.

Pius IX added: "Do you know what you did today? You almost killed the Pope. What would the world have said, especially the enemies of the Church? How they would have rejoiced over the fact that the Mortara child himself had killed the Pope! Now, kiss the ground."

Edgardo obeyed without opening his lips.

"That is not enough", continued His Holiness. "Now make a cross on the floor with your tongue." The young religious promptly carried out this order too.

Then, addressing those present, the Pope said: "Do you see what it means to be a religious? The only thing that religious must do or know is to obey. Now get up, my son, and go in peace!" And he tenderly blessed his protégé with a heavenly smile.

This is how the great Pontiff cared for the eternal fate of that soul, which was so precious in his sight, because it had cost, as he used to say, "the blood of our God". In this way his spiritual director and novice master was enabled to instruct and train him better in holy humility, the queen and mother of the manliest virtues, the mother of the most illustrious saints.

This lesson was deeply etched in the young student's memory and heart, to perfume his future.

Thus, the first years of his life in the cloister were spent, passing smoothly and quietly in the Eternal City of the popes, the new Jerusalem, in the shadow of Saint Peter's dome and of the papal tiara, under the warm, refreshing sun of Divine Providence, and the paternal affection of Pius IX. They were divided between the study of knowledge and the spiritual exercises of religious life, confirmed and expanded by the salutary counsels and appropriate teachings of his angelic Protector and Father in Christ.

Revenge attempted and thwarted

Nevertheless, this peaceful, serene prospect was darkening. Gloomy black clouds were forming, and a destructive storm could be seen approaching in the distance. One could sense tremendous disaster, but above this scene a consoling figure appeared. The good Jesus, alongside His vicar on earth, repeated, with a divinely beautiful gesture, words that were sweet and pleasant as nectar and honey: "Ego sum, noli timere" (Fear not, for I am with you) (Is 43:5). "Confidite, ego vici mundum" (Be of good cheer, I have overcome the world) (Jn 16:33).

On October 18, 1870, in the evening, in one of the moments of spare time allowed by the rule, the young man, in his blessed cell, hung a portrait of his angelic Protector. He placed the portrait in a frame and on the back he wrote the following incisive words: "Portrait of my Father and Protector in Christ, Pope Pius IX, *Pontifex Maximus*, to whom, after God, I must be grateful for all that I am by the grace of heaven. Saint Peter in Chains, October 18, 1870."

That memory, that inner movement that led his hand to trace the words just recorded, was a warning from the Lord. He was preparing the young man so that he would not succumb in the fierce battle that Hell was about to unleash, so as to make vain and useless all the work of grace and to plunge the sword of sorrow into the noble, magnanimous heart of Pius IX.

He had just finished writing the last word, when the Most Reverend Father Santini, his master and director, appeared in his cell. The priest announced a visit by the *questore* (chief of police), who wished to speak to him alone to discuss an issue of the greatest importance.

Very mixed feelings of astonishment and distrust accumulated in the student's soul. Accompanied by his master, he went without delay to the designated place, where Signor Berti, chief of police, was waiting for him. Meanwhile, he submissively listened to the counsels, adapted to the circumstances, that his prudent director was giving him.

While Father Santini waited in the vestibule of the hall with another gentleman who was accompanying Signor Berti, the following exchange took place between the latter and Edgardo.

SIGNOR BERTI: I must inform you that your father, with tears in his eyes, contacted the political authorities, so that they might convince you to pay a visit to your family.

EDGARDO: Allow me, Officer, to express my astonishment to see that a visit to my family is requested of me, when recently my father paid me a visit here, with the greatest affection.

SIGNOR BERTI: It is a reward and a satisfaction that public opinion demands from you, as they have never ceased to protest against the horrific abuses committed by the Pope twelve years ago, to the detriment of the parental authority.

EDGARDO: What satisfaction do they still want from me, even if it were legitimate, now that my father has visited me, and we conversed with the greatest affection, parting after I gave him several gifts as a testimony of the love I profess for my whole family and particularly for my beloved parents?

SIGNOR BERTI: I repeat that a visit to your family is demanded. Public opinion will not be satisfied in any other way.

EDGARDO: I do not have to be concerned about public opinion, given that, as I am on good terms with my family, I have nothing on my conscience. That public of which you speak cannot claim any satisfaction from me.

SIGNOR BERTI: I repeat that, for your own good and for that of the community to which you belong, you must pay this visit.

EDGARDO: Officer, I feel obliged to inform you that, for many substantial reasons that I refrain from pointing out, I am determined not to set foot in my family's lodgings. The visit that my father paid is public and known to all, as it is public and known to all that we parted with true affection. Therefore, there is no reason why I should go to visit my family, and I will not do it.

Signor Berti repeated again the same things, this time in an openly threatening tone. Then he got up and left the young man, who saluted him with the sweet, tranquil serenity and calm conferred by the performance of his duty.

Reverend Father Santini and the superiors immediately realized what was happening. They saw in this official and in this absolutely arbitrary pressure a great danger to the personal safety of the student, whose soul would perhaps be in the most terrible danger. They decided that Edgardo himself should write directly to General Alfonso La Marmora, then lieutenant of King Vittorio Emanuele in Rome, to ask his protection and help against the serious harassment to which he was in danger of being exposed.

General La Marmora, very famous and well known for his military campaigns and martial prowess, was one of the most powerful supporters and promoters of Italian unity, which he had always regarded as the most beautiful ideal of his life. Nonetheless, he was an honest and virtuous man, who did not acknowledge the temporal power exclusively inasmuch as that was irreconcilable, in his view, with the coveted national unity. In short, he was a moderate Italian, the only individual who, in that baleful time of stormy, disastrous policies, could present himself as "tolerable" alongside a Pope who had been so unjustly and barbarically dethroned. The Pope appealed not to the court of men but to the tribunal of God; the Catholic world fell silent and was resigned to the brutality of the fact once accomplished, to the tyranny of force, hoping that the force of divine law might one day punish the vile, disloyal invaders.

La Marmora was therefore a man whose moderation had to be, for the poor young man, a guarantee in such critical circumstances. A petition was drafted, which was signed by Edgardo himself, and was sent straight to the general through official channels.

On the same day, the cleric was accompanied by the Reverend Father Giuseppe Mariani, of the same Order, a very respectable religious, renowned both for his erudition and his virtues, a man who was truly capable, because of his fearless, decisive character, of directing, supporting, and encouraging the inexperienced professed religious. They appeared at the Palazzo della Consulta, the lieutenant's headquarters, to solicit the requested hearing immediately.

General La Marmora did not keep them waiting long. After greeting the two religious, he asked them to tell him in their own words what was going on. Hearing that the young man expressed well-founded fears and distrust because of harassment by those who wanted to oblige him arbitrarily to return to his family, he interrupted him to ask: "How old are you?"

"I will turn twenty this August."

"Then you are free [to make your own decisions]. Do you want to meet your parents?"

"No, sir, I do not want to, I do not have to, and I cannot. Why should I then? What do they want from me? A visit? My father just visited me, and we parted with cordial, affectionate words. They ask me for satisfaction? I am not required to give any to public opinion, which I have never failed in any of my duties, so it cannot demand anything from me. If they demand that I annul, personally and after the fact, as though in revenge, what Pius IX did twelve years ago, if they demand that I return to my family so as to deny my faith and to abandon the holy state of life that I have just embraced, I protest a thousand times. I repeat that I will not go: I do not want to; I do not have to; I cannot."

"But you are free, and nobody can force you if you do not want to."

"*Signor Generale*, the press threatens me, invoking the use of force and violence by the authorities."

"Do not worry: I will order that no one may harass you, and I will take you under my protection."

With these words he left the room, amiably bidding his two guests farewell.

The religious left quite satisfied, and Mortara would always remember the promise of generous protection that the brave soldier granted him at such a critical moment.

General La Marmora promised more than he could give, however, because he was influenced by people more intransigent than he, and there were plenty of reasons to be wary and take precautions.

In those same days, the Reverend Father Donzella, of the Order of Saint Benedict, arrived at Saint Peter in Chains. He resided at Saint Paul Outside the Walls and was the brother of Father A. Donzella, a fellow student of Edgardo. Informed of what had happened between the chief of police and the young man, he offered to talk to the Most Reverend Father Pisciatelli, Abbot of Saint Paul. Indeed, the *questore* was a close friend of Father Pisciatelli. Father Donzella would be able to converse with Signor Berti, in the company of Father Pisciatelli, in order to get him to desist from arbitrariness and violence, respecting at least the much-vaunted principle of freedom of conscience.

In fact, the two eminent, wise, and illustrious Benedictine fathers did so. The result of their meeting with Signor Berti was the relaxation of an already very tense situation. Don Pio could now count on more benign, conciliatory measures.

We cannot help mentioning this event as a testimony of deep gratitude to these venerable fathers.

Flight and emigration

Meanwhile, however, the liberal and antipapal press made a fuss, demanding provisions and energetic measures to "liberate" the one whom Pius IX had "seized".

None of this went unnoticed in Saint Peter in Chains. Among the other news reaching the ears of the fathers each day, the item that stood out was that the Italian police were watching every step taken by Edgardo and his venerable superiors. Every night, a picket of gendarmes was sent in front of the church to foil any attempt to escape.

That being the case, the only means of safety available, and therefore necessary, was flight: eluding the surveillance of the guards. This was precisely the decision made by the superiors, entrusting the project to the expert skills of the aforementioned Father Giuseppe Mariani. He was responsible for accompanying Edgardo during his emigration to Austrian Tyrol.

At ten o'clock in the evening before October 22, 1870, Father Mariani and the professed, both disguised as laymen, bid farewell to their confreres at Saint Peter in Chains.

Edgardo could barely hold back the tears. He knelt at the feet of the Most Reverend Father General Don Alberto Passari, the Most Reverend Father Don Agostino Bardagni, and his beloved master and spiritual director, Don Luigi Santini. All these, with their eyes wet with tears, gave their most affectionate blessing to the young traveler, who was entrusted, as a new Tobias, to his loyal, intrepid Raphael.

After bidding farewell to the Divine Majesty in the tabernacle, the two men, armed with the sign that distinguishes Christians, fervently prayed to Saint Peter, Saint Augustine, and Saint Agnes. They passed through a secondary side door of the *Canonica*—as the monasteries of the Canons are called—and made their way to the central train station, in Termini Square, to take the international train leaving at 11:00 P.M.

Once they arrived there, Father Mariani advised his protégé to assume a casual demeanor that would remove all suspicion. Then, without delay, he went to make the usual arrangements for the departure, while the young man waited for his return.

He returned shortly after. With his usual aplomb, he said with a smile: "You know, I just saw your father here. Take heart; you are with me; have no fear. Wear these black glasses and take this cigar. Even if you do not light it, keep it in your mouth."

A sudden shiver shook the poor fugitive, who was trembling all over. However, the presence, serenity, and unalterable good humor of his traveling companion supported the young man, just as Raphael's words and gestures supported and encouraged the young Tobias when he was about to be devoured by an enormous fish.

It is not known how or in what way, but even though that railway station, which was still temporary, was not very spacious, Edgardo did not see his father, nor did the latter meet him. Divine Providence, which never abandons those who hope and trust in it, visibly intervened.

The signal for departure was given; one could hear the whistle, then the roar of the locomotive. The train swayed and then set off. Becoming aware of the friendly smile that his dear Raphael was showing him, our Tobias brightened, and in the depths of his heart he repeated the words of the inspired psalmist: "Benedictus Dominus qui non dedit nos in captionem dentium eorum" (Blessed be the Lord, who has not given us as prey to their teeth) (Ps 124:6).

The travelers had not reached the end of their terrors, however. Upon arriving at Foligno, around midnight, they got off the train and went to the inn at the railway station to recover and to eat some food.

Across from the table at which they sat, two individuals were talking and drinking beer. Their untidy appearance, excited eyes, and violent, frantic gestures did not bode well for their character and profession. Most likely, they were two avid, resentful anticlericals or antipapists, or, as they were then called, "clergyphobes".

The two religious caught the drift of their conversation and clearly heard these words, which almost made Edgardo lose his temper: "Do you know what is happening? The father of the famous Mortara child is in Rome. He is in talks to get the authorities to force his son to return home. You know, it seems the young man emigrated abroad, eluding police surveillance, and they are now searching for him. It seems that this shameful evasion is the work of the Jesuits."

There is no need to describe here the terrible impression that this conversation produced on the already agitated soul of the fugitive. As though to ask for help, he gave his faithful guide a meaningful look. The intelligent, shrewd mentor, without making a fuss, having recommended that his protégé stay calm and keep the presence of mind necessary to avoid discovery, took part in the conversation with those two characters. He cleverly changed the subject, so that they completely forgot the issue of young Mortara's escape.

From Foligno to Ancona, Bologna, and Padua, the two travelers followed their route without further incident. Everywhere they went completely unnoticed. Although sometimes Edgardo, so susceptible even at that age, as in his childhood, showed fear or expected some harassment or violence, a friendly smile or a vigorous pat on the shoulder by his incomparable Raphael soon dissipated the clouds and reestablished calm in the sensitive young man.

When they arrived in Ala, the railroad station in the Austrian Tyrol, Edgardo raised his hands and eyes to Heaven, while a flash of sudden joy brightened his face. He exclaimed: "Blessed be God, I am finally out of danger!"

Those words were an echo and an unconscious but faithful reflection of the sigh of paternal affection that Pius IX breathed, in the presence of the whole papal court, when he was informed of the escape of his fortunate son. "Let us thank God, because now Mortara has left Italy!" These were his exact words, the meaning of which is quite natural and very clear.

Returning to his house and family would have been for him an occasion of apostasy. He would have abandoned his holy vocation and the Catholic faith, causing the eternal ruin of his soul!

Now the young man, full of joy, could exclaim, along with the inspired cantors and poets of his ancestors, when they left Egypt and crossed the Red Sea: "I will sing to the Lord, for he has triumphed gloriously" (Ex 15:1).

Exile

Our travelers now walked on Austrian soil, and, in particular, in blessed, happy Tyrol, which was still faithful to God, to its emperor, and to the fatherland, three words that form the motto of its flag. This Tyrol, so famous in history, so brave and heroic, such a zealous and ardent defender of its freedom and independence, flaunts with legitimate pride the trophies and crowns won by Andreas Hofer, its Hercules and its brave, invincible Achilles against the Jacobins of the tyrannical invader Napoleon Bonaparte. This Tyrol is famous for its faith, lived according to the true Tradition, for its irreproachable integrity, for its loyal, noble sincerity, and for its adamant, constant adherence to the throne of Saint Peter and the center of Catholicism. In this cheerful, peaceful land Edgardo spent the first two years of his exile.

Italy rejected him; Austria, its eternal, implacable rival—whose emperor glories in the title of "Apostolic Majesty"—welcomed and hosted him.

Divine Providence had prepared in advance and strewn roses on this path of emigration. Pater Johann Chrysostom Mitterrutzner, Canon Regular of the Lateran of the monastery of Neustift (Novacella in Italian), near Brixen (Bressanone), in Austrian Tyrol, had done his theological studies in Rome, earning a doctoral degree on June 21, 1846, the same day on which the Catholic world greeted Pius IX, the Vicar of Christ. He returned to the Eternal City in 1870, as a theologian for the Vatican Council and secretary to Monsignor Fessler, the secretary-general of the council.

This Canon, currently official director of the Imperial Royal Institute of Brixen, was famous for his learning and even more for his virtues. His venerable white hair reflected all the beauty of his soul and the purity and loftiness of his merits. He had met the Mortara child at Saint Peter in Chains, and from then on he had favored him with an affection inseparable from the esteem and veneration he harbored for the great Pontiff, the child's Protector and Father.

Father Mariani, on behalf of the superiors general in Rome, entrusted his beloved Tobias to this distinguished theologian, an erudite scholar and a respectable, worthy religious.

One cannot describe the intense, pleasant surprise that the unexpected presence of the two religious who had fled from "united" Italy produced in the soul of that venerable gentleman. He immediately introduced them to the Most Reverend Father Abbot of Neustift, Pater Dominik Irschara. Informed of everything, the latter tenderly embraced the young emigrant, offering him the most generous hospitality.

A few days later, the Reverend Father Mariani left for Rome, after entrusting Edgardo to the paternal and noble care of Father Mitterrutzner. From then on, the Tyrolean priest adopted him as a son in Christ, professing the most expansive affection for him, which never diminished.

Meanwhile, the godless enemies of the papacy, frustrated in their criminal plans, poured out through the freethinking press all the gall and poison of their satanic hatred for the Church, the Pope, and the religious orders, which were guilty of having instilled in the soul of the fugitive Mortara "principles", as they wrote, "that are totally opposed to the legitimate feelings of nature". Disappointed by the behavior of the young man, whom they depicted as a prisoner of executioners in religious habits, they vented the bitterness of their frustration. Once again all the old lies and falsehoods were trotted out.

The professed religious then took up his pen to defend the Church and his holy Protector Pius IX, by composing a written protest in which he claimed his freedom of conscience; it was published by Catholic newspapers in Italy, France, and Belgium. People were completely unaware of the young emigrant's haven, however.

Secluded in the strictest incognito, he took the name of Paolo Mazzarelli, devoting himself to the study of sacred theology, taught by Pater Franz Bole; of Hebrew, which he learned from the illustrious expert Herr Babe; and of German and other languages, to which he was introduced by his beloved protector and confrere, the Reverend Father Mitterrutzner.

On December 31, 1871, he took solemn vows at the hands of the Most Reverend Abbot of Neustift, who had been delegated by the Most Reverend Father Abbot General of the Order, Don Passeri. He then pursued his studies of the sacred sciences, in which he was subjected to the usual examinations in the presence of an eminent theologian and outstanding doctor. This was His Excellency Vincent Gasser, Bishop of Brixen, renowned for his erudition and virtues both in Austria and in Rome, who honored the protégé of Pius IX with a special affection.

In 1872, by order of the superiors, he moved from Austria to France, to the Diocese of Poitiers. The Bishop of that place, eminent in every respect, Monseigneur Pie, sensing the desire of Pius IX, had undertaken the construction of a new house for the Canons Regular of the Lateran at Our Lady of Beauchêne. He had received the necessary funding from the Most Excellent Lords Marquises of Rochejacquelein.

Monseigneur Pie, who later became a cardinal, had understood the intentions of Pius IX. The Pope, congratulating him in an Apostolic Brief on the completed construction, had commended to him his modest, unworthy protégé. Monseigneur Pie always had a deep affection for the young theologian: he addressed and treated him as a very dear son.

Edgardo dedicated the years 1872 to 1873 to the continuation of his theological studies. In these he was directed, together with his classmate Don A. Donzella, by the above-mentioned Reverend Father Mariani. He passed the required examinations to earn academic degrees under the presidency of the illustrious Monseigneur Pie. Other members of the committee were the Reverend Father Schrader and other Jesuit Fathers, who ran the theological college established in Poitiers by the same Bishop.

In those same years, he received, from the hands of the illustrious Bishop, minor and major orders. On December 20, 1873, when he was almost twenty-two and a half, thanks to an age dispensation of twenty months granted by the Pontiff, he received priestly ordination from the same Bishop. After a few days, through His Eminence the Nuncio of His Holiness Pius IX, the young man who was no longer Edgardo but Don Pio Maria, was honored by a Brief from the Supreme Pontiff. We cannot help transcribing and translating it, because we consider it the final step in the work of divine goodness and the greatest of the graces and favors granted by the immortal Pontiff. Here is the literal translation of the aforementioned Brief:

To my very beloved son Pio Maria Mortara, Canon Regular of the Lateran, at Our Lady of Beauchêne, Cerizay, Pius IX, Pope. Beloved son, Greetings and Our Apostolic Blessing.

We are delighted that your wishes, which are also Ours, are finally fulfilled. We rejoice that you, who were called to follow more closely in Christ's footsteps in a religious Family, were destined also for the priestly ministry. It is now time that, according to the decrees and orders of your superiors, you help to defend, strengthen, and spread His kingdom, and place yourself, as far as you are able and according to the circumstances, at the service of the spiritual well-being of your neighbors.

Moreover, we do not doubt that charity has been abundantly poured out into your heart—charity that must be continually increased by the One who is its very source—when for the first time you offered the divine Sacrificial Victim, which you renew every day. Nor do We doubt that you have remembered and remember us every time you offer the Holy Sacrifice.

Therefore, We congratulate you and wish you a daily increase in virtues and graces. Meanwhile, as a pledge of heavenly favors and as proof of Our paternal benevolence, with the greatest affection, We give you Our Apostolic Blessing.

Rome, at Saint Peter's, February 5, 1874, in the twenty-eighth year of our Pontificate.

                                        Pius IX, Pope

The words, congratulations, and fatherly blessings contained in this letter need no further comment. They complete the work of grace, so generous with the fortunate son of the Israelites. They show, to the highest degree, the benevolent indulgence of the angelic Pius IX. They are an inexhaustible source of strength and solace for Don Pio; they set the program for his whole life; they will perfume his future, will make his bitter trials bearable, and will be sufficient to support him in the fiercest battle. These words, accompanied by the signature of the Pontiff, whom Don Pio venerates and to whom, as a saint, he prays, are like a sacred relic for him, alongside the statuette of Saint Agnes and the gold medal that he received from the Holy Father himself. Don Pio sees in them the hand of Pius IX, always ready to bless him. With them in his heart and on his lips, he resolves to exhale his last breath, to go to face God—as he hopes—beside his holy Protector in Heaven.

As a result of his studies and of other trials and moral sufferings, a state of prostration together with a general excitement of the nervous system took possession of Don Pio. By order of the doctors, he had to give his mind some rest and engage in a series of physical exercises. It was a terrible ordeal, given his great propensity to speculative activities. The trial was mitigated, however, by the consolations provided by his religious confreres and by the blessings sent to him by His Excellency Monseigneur Pie, who cared for him like a father. Moreover, the blessing by Pius IX exhorted him to be patient during the time of this thorny trial.

On February 7, 1878, Don Pio wept, along with the Catholic world, over the loss of that great Pontiff, whom he revered and loved as a father. His deep sorrow would have been inconsolable had he not had the interior conviction that this great Pope, to whom Saint Malachy [allegedly] attributed the motto *Crux de Cruce* (Cross from the Cross), had flown like a white dove to the heavenly heights to receive the palm of victory and the beautiful crown of roses that he had earned as a martyr in the dwelling place of Christ and of His Church, which he had governed so wisely and piously for almost thirty-two years.

Among the many garlands and precious wreaths that adorn and embellish the glorious tomb of the Pontiff of the Immaculate and of the *Syllabus*, posterity will also notice the modest violet of his unworthy protégé, a purple flower placed there with the most tender and filial gratitude.

That same year, in order to obtain for him a little relief from his sufferings, the superiors transferred Don Pio to the residence of Mattaincourt in the Vosges (France), where he dedicated himself to preaching, despite the illness that afflicted him.

The rather sudden death of his good protector, the illustrious and Most Excellent Monseigneur Pie, Bishop of Poitiers, who for Don Pio was like another Pius IX, aggravated his sufferings.

Shortly before that, the much appreciated Father Mariani passed away in Mattaincourt; he had been superior of that house, the master and director of Don Pio, who owed so much to him.

In 1880, the application of the famous article 7 of the anti-Christian law by Jules Ferry resulted in the violent expulsion of foreign Canons Regular who were residing in France. Don Pio, then living in Marseilles to take sea baths prescribed by the doctors, found himself in a very critical situation, because his name was so hated by the enemies of the Church, and furthermore he was a foreigner and was unable to move to more distant lands. In such painful circumstances, while maintaining the strictest incognito, he was welcomed and hosted in Rome by the excellent and distinguished Marcorelles ladies, whom he had met earlier.

Those devout, charitable ladies had a kind of devotion to Pius IX, and as a sign of their reverence for him, they welcomed Don Pio with the greatest kindness and courtesy. Indeed, the nobility, detachment, and spirit of Christian self-denial that these excellent ladies showed during the violent crisis that Don Pio was going through, surpass all praise. He had to stay in bed for fifty-eight days, barely able to eat any food while in the grip of strong nervous agitation. Don Pio can never praise enough the support that he received from the ladies or thank them for it. A mother and sisters full of love would have not done more.

This trial was considerably alleviated by the presence of the Reverend Father Pardini, the Visitator of the Order sent by the Most Reverend Father General. It was also soothed by the benevolent, delicate attentions he received from the Most Reverend Father Abbot of the Benedictines, from the nuns of the Buon Soccorso (two of whom assisted him every night), and finally from an illustrious Bishop. The latter honored him with a visit, and granted him all sorts of spiritual favors, authorizing him to have an altar and to celebrate Holy Mass in his own room. The good ladies did everything possible so that the patient would lack no spiritual consolation.

On March 11, 1880, the next-to-last day of a novena that was being celebrated in honor of the glorious Saint Joseph for the health of the sick, Don Pio, who had prepared himself for the death that a famous holy priest had foretold to him with a precise date and time, began for the first time to take a little more food. A few days later the patient got up, starting a slow but visible and sure recovery.

To facilitate this convalescence, his superiors arranged his transfer to Brixen, where he had lived until eight years before. Needless to say, he was received by Father Mitter-rutzner and by those good Canons with incredible affection and brotherly kindness.

Meanwhile, at the suggestion and initiative of His Excellency Giovanni Simeoni, Secretary of State of His Holiness Pius IX, Jaime Catalá y Albosa, Bishop of Cádiz, Spain, welcomed in his diocese Don Barsotti and Don Donzella, together with Don Pio, who were sent by Father General Santini. They settled in San Fernando or Isla de León, thanks to the collaboration of the excellent and outstanding ladies of the De Landa family.

Don Pio remained four years in Andalusia, until, in 1884, by order of his superiors, he made a journey on the Iberian Peninsula, to advertise and spread his Order, whose restoration was starting in Spain under the wise direction of the Reverend Father Barsotti.

Many travels and trials of all kinds followed, which increased the sufferings that continued to plague Don Pio. He finally settled in the northern provinces of Spain, and in particular in the Basque region, which seemed the most suitable for the desired objective of building a new house and founding a novitiate. Don Pio was welcomed with the greatest kindness by the illustrious Bishop of Vitoria, who showed interest in an idea Don Pio proposed to him: to undertake a foundation in the diocese. As this prelate had planned to set up a minor seminary in the building of the famous University of Oñate, through Don Pio he offered the Most Reverend Father General of the Canons Regular the direction of that seminary.

Consequently, Father Santini commissioned Father Barsotti, then superior of the house in San Fernando, to move to Vitoria to discuss this matter with the illustrious Bishop.

A few days later, Fathers Barsotti and Mortara met with the prelate. Father Barsotti understood the state of the negotiations to build the seminary in Oñate, which were still pending and not easy to resolve. He therefore arrived with special powers conferred on him by the Bishop. Thanks to his intellectual dexterity, the obstacles were overcome. The minor seminary was finally inaugurated on November 2, 1884. Father Barsotti was appointed rector and superior, and Fathers Mortara and Menais were to teach the basic subjects.

In the following years, the number of personnel kept increasing, both in the seminary and in the community. It was the illustrious Bishop's desire that the Order of the Canons Regular should "identify with the future of the famous university". Therefore, the Reverend Father Barsotti agreed with the other fathers on starting a temporary novitiate of the Order within that university. The building, though, was not large enough to accommodate so many people. A new house had to be built exclusively for the members of the Order, and then a church that would have greater capacity than the small university chapel, for the requirements of divine worship.

They lacked the necessary funds to carry out such a large project, which involved considerable expenses. The fathers put all their trust in the Sacred Heart of Jesus, to whom they unanimously decided to dedicate the new house and church. Since Father Mortara, such a beloved son of Divine Providence, he who bore the highly revered name and memory (along with the blessings) of the great Pius IX, was the one on whom the accomplishment of such a holy work depended, they all decided to put him in charge of the mission of appealing to the charity of good people so as to collect the necessary funds.

Father Mortara dedicated himself to this mission (appealing to the charity of the Spaniards, and in particular of the good Basques), in the midst of struggles of every

kind and despite his poor health. The new house of the
Sacred Heart was built and dedicated; it was inhabited by
a community of twenty-eight persons, led by the abovementioned Father Barsotti. Father Mortara continued to
appeal to the charity of the people in order to build Sacred
Heart Church next to the house. Construction had already
advanced considerably—a monument to what the good
Spaniards' love for Jesus Christ can accomplish.

As for Father Mortara, he has only one desire, one vow:
that he might have the joy of completing such a noble,
holy mission, directed to the greater glory of God, to establish and spread His apostolic Order, which was once so
famous and popular in Spain; that he might have the
hope that such an extraordinary mission will not be frustrated; that the blessings of Pius IX might not prove useless, nor the labors and trials of his life fruitless; that he
might, at the moment of death, repeat in his heart the
words of Saint Paul: "His grace toward me was not in
vain" (1 Cor 15:10). May this be his last heartbeat, when
he will plunge into the divine and adorable Heart of Jesus,
which is his strength and his life, and must be his eternal
fascination in the heavenly homeland.

A look back

A natural and legitimate curiosity will prompt those who
read these humble pages to inquire about the life of that
girl from whom Father Pio Mortara received the water of
Baptism. Moreover, readers will want to know what happened to his family. We will answer in a few lines.

As for the good Anna Morisi, who baptized the Mortara child, I already wrote earlier, if I am not mistaken,
that when the abduction took place by explicit order of

Pius IX, the poor girl was in trouble and had to leave Bologna to escape violent harassment and reprisals.

In the trial that took place in 1860 against the Most Reverend Father Feletti, General Inquisitor in Bologna, who had been charged with carrying out the Supreme Pontiff's orders with respect to the Mortara child, it was recorded that Anna Morisi had returned to her birthplace, Tossignano, near Bologna. There she settled after marrying in the Church.

The Supreme Pontiff Pius IX spoke more than once, in Edgardo's presence, about the girl. Presumably the good Pope did not fail to take an interest in her compromised future and sent her some aid.

Father Mortara then completely lost track of the Morisi woman. Despite all the investigations that he initiated and the reports that he requested to find out where she had taken refuge and what the circumstances of her life were, he could never discover anything certain or obtain any satisfactory news.

May the infinitely merciful God, who deigned to choose, among so many others who were wandering in the darkness of error, the helpless Jewish child, reserve an eternal reward for that girl, who was the instrument of grace for him, and who, without his being aware, bore him spiritually in God. Don Pio ardently wishes this, and he will always regard Anna Morisi as his mother in the supernatural order.

As for the Mortara family, we must report now that the famous abduction was not the cause of their ruin, and did not sink them into poverty, contrary to what the enemies of the Church and of the Pope's temporal power are fond of repeating, using these pretexts to destroy him. Instead, this sequestration was the beginning, if not precisely of an enrichment, then at least of a well-being that they had not enjoyed before. Indeed, generous donations were sent to Signor and Signora Mortara by those who pretended hypocritically to lament their lot and their misfortune. The name Mortara acquired unexpected celebrity. In the commerce, in the industry, and in the other activities to which the Mortara brothers devoted themselves, this name was a sort of very prestigious label that could not help attracting remarkable material advantages.

Of the eleven children, fruit of the union of Signor and Signora Mortara, two lived only a few months. Riccardo, the eldest, joined the army and became an officer. Then he returned to his family.

After the death of their father, Salomone, Augusto earned a doctorate in law. The other three brothers worked in different fields of commerce and industry. The three sisters, after finishing their education, settled into honest marriages.

In 1872, Don Pio received the very sad news of his beloved father's death, which occurred in circumstances too painful and unpleasant to report in these pages. May the infinite, inexhaustible goodness of God deign to look on him with affection and mercy!

The disconsolate, elderly mother is still alive, having almost reached the age of seventy. She is very strict and observant in her Jewish religion and wants the Law of Moses to be observed in her family. She is full of sentiments of boundless trust in God, whose name she always has on her lips. With regard to religion, her three daughters, Erminia, Ernesta, and Imelda, are true portraits of their mother.

As a result of the political events that took place in 1870 and of the very critical and delicate situation in which Don Pio found himself, correspondence with his family ceased. He was able to resume it only in 1876. Since then, between

Don Pio and all his siblings, but in particular between him and his beloved, adored mother, whose portrait he always keeps in sight, a tender, filial, affectionate correspondence has been exchanged.

This poor lady, who, in the famous Mortara case was and always will be the lady of suffering, is adored by all her children and loves them all deeply, but has a preference, as is natural, for her "son of sorrow", Edgardo. He unwillingly caused her many tears and much bitterness.

A mother is always a mother, and those words of the divine Suffering Servant, "Let this chalice pass from me", are a legitimate part of her heart and nature and justify every sorrow, especially that of a mother.

In the thirty years he has spent away from home, Don Pio met his beloved mother only twice, in a quick, fleeting way, during his forced exile in foreign lands. She seems to think only about him. She is also very afflicted because her health is not very robust. She wishes that she had wings to fly close to her beloved son, waiting, as she said, for a day to come when God might "help and favor her".

More than once the priest tried to talk to his mother about Jesus, and to put her afflicted heart in contact with that of the adored Redeemer. The woman, however, would start crying, and what can one say to a weeping mother? What other response can one make but a respectful silence?

Don Pio, too, weeps with Jesus, secluded in His divine Heart. Yes, he weeps with Christ, who wept for the sisters of Lazarus and wept over Jerusalem.

Many times, unable to speak about Him to his mother, he speaks about his mother to Him, in particular when he offers the Holy Sacrifice of the altar and holds in his hands and places on his lips the pure Host, the holy Victim, the spotless Victim.

Don Pio's prayers and tears, it is true, are worth little, very little. They are, however, completed, elevated, and transfigured by the prayers and tears of so many generous souls. With him they beg the consoling light for his beloved mother. There are devout aspirations and good deeds that many brides of the spotless Lamb offer. Like innocent white doves, they surround the heavenly Beloved and plead, beg, and importune Him with their gestures and moans.

Ah, Don Pio lives by hope and knows that hope is never entirely frustrated: *spes non confundit.*

Don Pio hopes that his mother's good faith and natural piety will save her, as they saved the good Canaanite woman.

Don Pio believes and hopes in Jesus. Just as Saint Augustine, that great luminary of the Church, his great Father and Doctor, was the most productive fruit of the difficult sorrows and tears of his mother, Monica, so too may Don Pio's mother become a Catholic, to his joy, and a friend of Jesus, as the much-desired fruit of her son's tears. May he generate to the supernatural life of grace the one who gave him life and material light. After passing through this valley of tears, may their hearts, inseparably united, meet with the hearts of all those who pray with Don Pio. May they all lose themselves in the heart of God, on the heights of eternal and everlasting happiness!

The last word

Yes, after everyone busied himself about the famous Mortara case, after governments throughout Europe, after the great and the lowly, friends and enemies, the press, parliaments, clubs, in short, after everybody except Mortara himself has spoken about the case concerning him, it is just, fitting, and fair that Mortara himself should have the last word. The last word for our posterity of time, and not of nature, as the Scholastics would say. Last, not in the sense of definitive and decisive, nor in the sense of authoritative. Last, not to settle or decide a question that has long since been finished and exhausted. Last only in the sense of later in time, which is exactly the writer's concern. May this word be a modest flower offered to the glorious and blessed memory of Pius IX. May it be a testimony of perpetual gratitude to the Catholic Church and to the apostolic Order to which Don Pio has the honor of belonging, to this illustrious Order that raised and educated him in the sound, true doctrine that he is preparing to set forth.

Of course, we do not seek here to develop a thesis or to write a dissertation, which would bore the benevolent readers with texts and citations, in a wearisome labyrinth of difficult, abstract speculations. Ours is merely a word that concentrates, as though in a prism, as though in a sketch, and in miniature, what other, more competent writers have presented in learned, erudite pages, which those who seek more detailed arguments can read.

Our objective is to demonstrate briefly and succinctly that in the famous sequestration of the child, Pius IX, as Head of the Catholic Church and visible Vicar of Christ, made use of one of his rights and did his duty. And he did so while relying on the eternal ideals and the inalterable judgments of both natural and divine law.

First of all, let us summarize the facts once again. They are simple, we have already mentioned them, but, as the ancient adage says, *Repetita juvant.* (Repeating does good.) In the year of grace 1858, Pius IX was at the same time Pope and King: he was the spiritual head of Catholics, the pastor of pastors, the successor of Saint Peter, and a temporal prince. He was the Vicar of Christ and at the same time sovereign of the Papal States, invested with legislative, judiciary, and executive power. In short, he was a king in all the far-reaching connotations of the word, as are other kings and sovereigns in their respective States. Indeed, he was a king more than they, given that the political form of monarchy has been integrally adopted in the Patrimony of Saint Peter since time immemorial.

Signor and Signora Mortara, as Jews, were really and truly subjects of Pius IX, to whom they owed respect, obedience, and submission by law in matters of religion and by law and in fact in civil matters.

Among the laws then in force in the Papal States there was one by virtue of which it was severely and unconditionally forbidden for Jews to hire young Christian women as servants. This was to prevent violations and abuses and the excesses of an inopportune zeal, which the Church and the popes have always disapproved and condemned, particularly in the not-very-distant days of Benedict XIV.

Church history in Spain offers numerous peremptory proofs of this. Notwithstanding this law, the Mortaras, for the precise and specific purpose that the other servants might observe the letter of the law of complete rest on the Sabbath, took into their household the young Anna Morisi.

The child Edgardo was seriously ill; the doctors had lost all hope of saving him. His parents, confronted with all the most unequivocal signs of a fatal end of the incident, abandoned themselves to a desperate sorrow. The child was on the point of taking his last breath; only a few moments more and he would be in Eternity. In short, in Scholastic terms, the child was *in articulo mortis*.

In such a terrible predicament, the Morisi woman, who had been appropriately instructed, knew her catechism well and the manner and form for administering the Sacrament of Baptism to a dying person. She took a glass of water, dipped her hand into it, and baptized the child in the ecclesiastical form of *Baptisma clinicorum*, in other words, Baptism of the sick, that is, *per aspersionem* (by sprinkling). It is a maternal provision of the Church in the case of imminent death.

And instead, shortly afterward, the child miraculously recovered and was completely restored to health. He remained thus for six years in his family without the young woman daring to tell anyone what had happened. God and she knew it, but no one else, not even Edgardo.

Divine Providence, nevertheless, interceded and intervened. A little brother of Edgardo found himself in the same situation; he too was in imminent danger of death. Although she was grieving and her friends pleaded with her, Anna Morisi refused to baptize Edgardo's little brother. She did not want to risk a repetition of the previous case. The poor baby died without having been regenerated by the saving waters. This was the occasion of grace upon which Anna revealed the incident with Edgardo to her friends and then, through her confessor, to the ecclesiastical authority.

The Supreme Pontiff was informed and gave instructions adapted to the circumstances. He charged the ecclesiastical authorities of Bologna to have recourse first to the most conciliatory means of persuasion. They proved useless. The subversive party, which was highly developed in Bologna, rebelled. By express order of the Supreme Pontiff, in his capacity as Vicar of Christ and as temporal sovereign and Prince, he proceeded to sequester the child. The executive power appeared in the house, solely and exclusively to prevent any open and violent resistance and rebellion. Pius IX had the child carried away and took charge of his education. Thanks to his paternal protection, Edgardo grew and made progress, remaining firm in the beliefs that were taught him. He then consecrated himself to God in the Order of Canons Regular of the Lateran.

This, in the briefest possible terms, is the famous Mortara case, which has been debated, argued, and discussed so much by all the means of publicity. The famous Catholic writer and polemicist Veuillot was quite right when he called it a "wearisome, troublesome question".

We arrive, therefore, at the last word. We will prove that both natural law and divine law sanction and fully justify the sequestration of the child, which took place on June 24, 1858, by supreme order of Pius IX.

Let us limit ourselves, first of all, to the natural law: What does it say with respect to parental authority over the education of children?

Because parents are the immediate principle of the child's existence—and, indirectly and mediately, of the soul created *ex nihilo* by God as the First Cause and the Sole Cause of intelligent substances—and since in every creature duties and rights are correlated, parents have the right and the duty to contribute, by themselves or with the help of others, to the material and moral development of their offspring.

Leaving aside the material part and limiting our attention to the moral part: parents have the duty to provide directly or indirectly for the development of the child's natural faculties, above all with regard to religion.

Speaking about the natural law, we must care for nature, not as it presently exists, that is, in its diminished or fallen state—or, as theologians would say, its "corrupted" state—but as it ought to be, as it came forth from the Creator's hands, in the state of integrity, as, again, theology would put it. Leaving aside the supernatural gifts that were not owed to it, let us consider nature as not yet contaminated

and stained by actual sin, born of that original or hereditary sin.

The natural law brings us back to these summits, on
which the sun of truth and original justice shines, consequently eliminating the transmission of error and vice from
father to son. This same natural law affirms that the parent
has the duty to know the truth and to practice virtue, and
to hand down both to his descendants.

Let us acknowledge provisionally that God wishes
to raise man to a supernatural order and that there is an
authority invested by God Himself with the power to
guide and direct him in this order. Then it is the right
of parents—and consequently their duty also—to keep in
mind this sublime destiny of their offspring. They must
guide and prepare them for this and then entrust them to
the higher authority established by God.

Yet in the present order of things, given nature as it
exists—namely, diminished and corrupted in its noblest
part, with the intellect liable to error and the will inclined
to vice—the archetypal, primordial ideas are and always
remain the same and identical. There are duties and rights
of the intellectual nature, even when the application
thereof is forcibly modified, and sometimes suspended by
the interference of free will, weakened by the habitual dis-
position to vice, in the theological development of man's
moral faculties.

In the present state of degraded nature, supposing that
the parents profess error and adhere to a false religion, they
likewise have the inescapable duty to embrace the true
religion and to educate their children in it. They themselves and their descendants must direct their steps toward
the supernatural order that God is free to establish.

If this supernatural order does, in fact, exist, and if there
is an authority invested with the power to direct men

toward this order, parents belonging to a false religion are subject to this spiritual authority *de jure*, in other words, by law. They are strictly and rigorously obliged to subject themselves to it, to respect its laws, and to obey its commands. This is true even if they are not subject to it *de facto*, that is, in the case in which they belong to another religion. Indeed, God does not want violence to be done to the creature's liberty; hence, the religious authority of the supernatural order established directly by God cannot be extended to those individuals who in fact (even if not by law) are not subject to it.

In this case, we have considered parenthood in the order of integral nature, that is, nature that is still intact and unspotted by sin, in the full possession of its rights and invested with the ability to fulfill its duties and to hand down this precious heritage to the offspring. Currently, in the order of fallen, degenerate, corrupted nature, even presupposing actual adherence to a true religion of the supernatural order directly established by God, parental authority is a diminished, fallen, and degenerate authority, like the nature in which it is rooted. In this situation its duties remain and are maintained with the same rigor, while its rights are rather hypothetical and apparent, and never—never, I say—do they or will they prescribe things opposed to truth and virtue, or against God's express will.

Until they have arrived at the full use of their moral faculties, the offspring follow their parents, being a part and complement of their substance. Of necessity, unfortunately, they will follow them also on the dark path of error and rebellious passions.

If, however, the child, glimpsing some rays of revealed truth, and feeling impulses and aspirations toward a supernatural good rising in his heart, decides to pursue this truth and this good, whose pure splendor he perceives from afar,

the parental authority must withdraw and bow respectfully before the dividing line that separates it from the
sacred rights of liberty. If it is unwilling to acknowledge the presence of the Deity, it will have to respect
at least the indisputable supremacy of human reason and
freedom, which no one, except God or the one who
represents Him, can subdue or shackle. Otherwise, the
intrusion of parental authority into this sacred, inviolable area would become despotism and barbarism. Parenthood as such must seek the true good of the offspring.
Otherwise it would become complicit in and responsible
by obligation for their eternal unhappiness.

In that case, the intervention of a higher authority
would be necessary from every perspective, and it matters little whether it is essentially distinct from the political
authority. This authority, by its nature and mission super-
seding parental authority, would have to defend the sacred
rights of freedom that had been outraged and barbarously,
despotically shackled. It would have to remove the child
from the unjust vexations, which are all the more fatal and
lamentable insofar as they affect the higher part of human
nature, preventing it from reaching and obtaining its eternal, immortal destiny.

And if this intervention, which, of course, would be
conciliatory and peaceful, did not obtain the desired result,
what would have to be the solution and conclusion of the
painful but necessary struggle between the two authorities, the private and the public; between the two powers,
the civil and the religious; between the two authorities, the
natural and the supernatural? Coercive force. There is no
other response. If action is not taken in this way, nothing
remains but disorder, confusion, and chaos.

Let us not tarry longer in discussing these theories, which
are abstract but of great importance. We do not want to

bore our readers, and we will descend to their application to the case about which we are concerned.

Let us first put things into the true perspective; then we will be generous toward our adversaries, limiting ourselves to the highly esteemed principle of "liberty".

The Catholic religion is the one true, supernatural religion; it is a society of a superior order, essentially distinct from civil society.

The Mortaras profess the Jewish religion, which is contradictory and surpassed by history.

Consequently, the parental authority of Signor and Signora Mortara is diminished, disabled, and is not in full possession of its rights, nor does it know its duties. Their duty is to embrace the true, Christian religion and to educate their children in it. It is an inescapable, absolute duty, against which it is not morally possible to be opposed.

The Mortaras are, however, free, and God respects their freedom and wants and commands men to respect it. Therefore, no one will oblige the Mortaras to abandon their religion to embrace the Catholic religion, and never, never did the Church think of imposing it by force.

Therefore, the children of the Mortaras, as the substantial emanation of them, as the ramification and complement of their being and existence, follow their parents on that same misguided, erroneous path. Until they have attained the full and complete exercise of their faculties, they will perforce be Jews, and no one will be allowed to impose on them any other beliefs whatsoever.

Once they have reached the age of reason and the full exercise of their moral faculties, however, they will be open to means of persuasion, and they can be drawn by the truth without any injury to the sacred rights of human liberty.

Nevertheless, the famous Mortara case was not about a Jewish child, but about an already baptized child, one baptized *in articulo mortis*, that is, on the point of taking

his final breath. These two circumstances must be emphasized, since they shed a strong light on this much-debated
problem.

At the point of death, when the organism is transformed,
disintegrates, and is corrupted, the child ceases to belong
to his parents. This disabled, broken being now belongs to
eternity and to God, and heads toward them.

Human parlance, which is both simple in itself and
exact and philosophical, regards this child as an isolated,
sequestered being and calls him "given up and abandoned"
by the doctors and the parents, who have now lost all hope
of saving him.

Now, precisely in that very solemn and terrible emergency, when he is about to enter into eternity, God's
infinite goodness takes possession of the soul of that child
who is now abandoned. God guides and impels the hand
of that girl, places her at the foot of the Cross of the divine
Redeemer, from whose pierced Heart flows and separates a drop of His adorable blood. Mixed with the baptismal water, this drop regenerates, purifies, and sanctifies
that soul, which men do not appreciate because they do
not know it; but God loves, predestines, and protects it
because it cost all the blood of God.

What rights can be asserted by the parents of the child
who has been abandoned by men and welcomed by God?
Who interfered here; who profaned the sacred power of
liberty; who did violence to the will of that child?

All the "blame", if "blame" there be, belongs to God.
There is no doubt that God's rights are superior to those of
parental authority, which in this case happens to be completely destitute even of merely apparent rights.

What the parents are neither able nor willing to give
the helpless child—in other words, truth, virtue, holiness in germinal form, Christ, God, and Paradise as an

inheritance—all this God gives him, and He gives it to him because He wants to. Here is a case where we can say, "Stat pro ratione voluntas." (He stands for a reason.) The divine will prevails over petty human reason.

Here parental authority is in a state of incapacity. If it has command of the child, then instead of truth—which, as Saint Augustine teaches so incisively and energetically, is "the life of the soul" (*animae vita veritas*)—it will give him the poison of error and with it eternal death and the principle of all evils.

This diminished parental authority, dispossessed of its rights and, in the case that concerns us, harmful to the child's eternal salvation, is replaced by the authority of the heavenly Father, who regenerates this poor child in the agonizing Heart of His adorable Son. God chooses this soul, takes it for Himself, justifies it, and claims it. Who would dare to ask God why?

The civil law in the state where the Mortaras lived, then, is explicit. It commands and prescribes the sequestration of a child when he is in danger of moral corruption by his parents.

Now the Mortara child finds himself precisely in this situation. He has reached the age of reason and is seven years old. He is Christian, Catholic, and as such is a child of God, brother of Christ, heir of Heaven. He does not know the God who revealed the law of grace; he is ignorant of Christ and of the Church founded by Him. Not only is he ignorant of all this, but he begins to detest it and to hate it, at least potentially. Instead of directing his steps toward Paradise, he is heading toward the abyss. What will be his situation with respect to his parents?

The dilemma is decisive. He will become an apostate, a wretch, a compulsory apostate, a tyrannized son who never comes to know what he is. And therefore, of necessity, he will remain an apostate. Or else he will come to know what he is and will refuse to adhere to the divine religion in which God incorporates him and will be freely, voluntarily apostate; and that would be a horrible crime.

Or else, he will come to know what he is and will want to follow God, who is calling him like Abraham and is inviting him to leave his land and his forefathers. What will his parents do then? The pen does not dare to relate it, but the imagination guesses and recoils in alarm.

In any case, this child is exposed to the greatest danger, at risk of the worst treatment by those who, instead of giving him, as they should *de jure*, the greatest good for man (the truth, holiness, and Heaven), inasmuch as they cannot *de facto*, they hurl him into the abyss of all evils.

We repeat: the civil laws in a Christian state are explicit in this case. The Mortara child must be separated from his parents.

Of course, if the gentler, more conciliatory measures do not obtain the hoped-for result, and if the moral perversion of the child is evident and inevitable, the laws justify, command, and prescribe sequestration.

And this is exactly what Pius IX did. He neither stole nor kidnapped a child from his parents, as the anti-Catholic press repeated tirelessly. After resorting to all possible methods of persuasion and conciliation, after proposing gentle, paternal measures to the parents, in view of the extreme and imminent danger incurred by the child's soul, which had been washed and cleansed by His precious blood, Pius IX proceeded to separate the child. He was then seven years old and had attained the use of reason. Therefore, he could have been the object of cruel treatment. He could have become, through a perverse, erroneous education, an apostate, a compulsory heretic, an enemy of Jesus and of His Church. Pius IX, an inspired genius, a guardian angel, an invincible and unvanquished Moses of the law of grace, understood what a soul is, a soul that costs the blood of God. He rescued this soul from Hell so as to restore it to the One who predestined and chose it, to Christ, the Son of the true God, the invisible Head of the Church.

Either you nullify the entire legal code, and with it the whole natural law, or you must acknowledge and confess that Pius IX rightly did a good deed in sequestering the Mortara child. He did not throw him into prison; he did not hand him over to merciless executioners; he did not cause him to sink into poverty: on the contrary, he placed him in the mystical Eden. He would teach him to love Jesus, so as then to be His minister and to sanctify his own soul and the souls of others.

How barbaric, therefore, Pius IX was, and how pious are those who accuse and slander him for having carried out the separation of the child, thus plunging his family into sorrow!

As for the facts and proofs that divine law offers us, we find in it judgments that are so decisive, so explicit, definitive, and overwhelming that we hardly dare to report them, given the extreme sensitivity, not to mention the crass, supine ignorance, of many Catholics who understand everything in their own way and measure God's works by their own restricted vision.

The divine Redeemer says:

Do not think that I have come to bring peace on earth; I have not come to bring peace, but a sword. For I have come to set a man against his father, and a daughter against her mother, and a daughter-in-law against her mother-in-law; and a man's foes will be those of his own household. He who loves father or mother more than me is not worthy of me; and he who loves son or daughter more than me is not worthy of me; and he who does not take his cross and follow me is not worthy of me. (Mt 10:34–38)

What? The God of peace and charity, the author and founder of the law of grace, the good and most sweet Jesus, the Lamb of God, whom Saint Paul identifies with "meekness and gentleness" (2 Cor 10:1), is the same one who uttered such terrible words, which seem to have no other purpose than to break up domestic tranquility at its foundations?

"Ah, no!" the great Pontiff Saint Gregory replies. "The same Divine Master who uttered these very forceful, explicit words also said, in speaking about matrimony: 'What God has joined together, let not man put asunder.' And through His Apostle, addressing spouses, He said to them: 'Husbands, love your wives, as Christ loves His Church.'" The holy Doctor continues:

> If we look closely, therefore, we can keep both precepts very well, on the one hand loving relatives and our neighbor; on the other hand hating spiritual enemies, those who obstruct us on the path of good and truth. We must flee from the latter and pay no attention to what they tell us or advise us.

Ecclesiastical law is very clear and precise in its decrees about the sons of the Israelites who, for any reason whatsoever, have received the Sacrament of Baptism. It truly takes all the bad faith of restless minds to call into question the right of Pius IX in the Mortara case.

Since it is not our purpose here to develop a theological thesis, we will limit ourselves to reporting that in the various decrees promulgated by Benedict XIV regarding the abovementioned cases, the conclusion is always the same:

"If there is danger of perversion"—as there almost always will be—"let the child be separated from his parents."

Note well that these canonical regulations make no mention of other kinder, more conciliatory measures, to which Pius IX, in contrast, had recourse; he ordered compulsory separation only after the gentler measures had failed.

Let us not linger anymore on the prescriptions of canon law developed and applied to the Mortara case by eminent theologians and experts. Their mouthpieces were, in the volcanic field of the press (which nowadays is a formidable power), in France *L'Univers*, headed by the great Veuillot, and in Spain *La Esperanza*, directed by Señores Hoz and Vildósola. This newspaper later on took the name *La Fe*, which is still in use. What took place in these newspapers happened in the Catholic press worldwide: the Baptism of a child moved the readers and prompted them to come to his defense.

How could it surprise anyone that both divine law and ecclesiastical law were so decisive and explicit in a matter concerning the eternal salvation of a soul and the duties that follow from it?

Louis Veuillot, whose memory we are pleased to mention, in one of those flashes of genius that for him were so natural and so sublime, hurled this harsh but well-deserved admonishment at the people who were in an uproar because of the Mortara child: "You have forgotten what Baptism is and do not know Christian doctrine." This prophetic utterance recalls the famous remark of the great Hermit of Bethlehem, the incomparable Saint Jerome, concerning the Second Council of Ephesus and what followed it: "The world awoke to find itself Arian."

In the Mortara case, which has been debated and discussed so much, the unexpected news was that Baptism and Christian doctrine had been forgotten.

Baptism is the spiritual regeneration of the soul. As Saint Thomas says so profoundly, it is the interior reflection of the face of Christ in the soul. Through the water, grace is communicated to the soul in view of Christ's merits, which are applied to the baptized person. From that moment on, the soul is regenerated: a term that is divinely expressive and exact and summarizes everything. The grace communicated to the soul by the merits of the divine Mediator gives it a new life, a new *being*, which has a supernatural character, superior to all that nature brings with it, and to all that results from it or is rooted in it. We are talking about a true, mysterious participation in the divine perfections. "You must be born anew", the Lord said to Nicodemus.

Through this grace, the soul, although sinful in Adam and because of Adam, is purified and reconciled in Christ and through Christ. Although it was a child of wrath and fire, the soul is elevated and exalted to the status of child and heir: heir of God and coheir of Christ, as Saint Paul puts it. With Him, and with other men who believe in Christ and in the One who sent Him, he will form from now on one body (*unum corpus*), just as he will participate by the same faith and by the same Baptism in the same Lord: *unus Dominus, una fides, unum baptisma*.

But the Church, according to the Apostle's preaching, is the Body of Christ, His continuation and His personification, endowed with the same divine, supernatural mission to "make disciples of all nations, baptizing them in the name of the Father and of the Son and of the Holy Spirit" (Mt 28:19). Christ loves the Church and for her sake handed Himself over to the executioners; God wanted the Church to be without blemish, so that she might be holy and immaculate. The Church has a visible head, the vicar of the invisible divine Captain; to him the Lord said, in the person of Peter, "You are Peter, and on this rock I will build my Church"; Christ ordered him to feed His lambs and His sheep. The Church has authority over this soul of the child who belongs to Jesus, over this soul that cost the life and the blood of God. The Church is charged to keep that soul safe and to give it "spiritual milk" as though to "newborn infants", as Saint Peter writes.

The child who cannot make use of reason is absolutely incapable of fulfilling this inescapable, sacred duty of knowing revealed truth and practicing gospel morality. The Church, therefore, his Mother in the order of grace, represented by the Shepherd of shepherds, the Supreme Pontiff, will fill the gap, will accomplish this mission, and will ensure the eternal future of this soul. She will do so by incorporating it into Christ and giving it the balm and heavenly nectar of faith and the love that will never fail.

This admirable, divine economy of grace is fully manifested and confirmed in the Mortara case. His soul, regenerated by Baptism, belongs to the Church of Christ more than to his parents, who have only indirect and accidental rights over his soul. Through the very blood that was the adorable price of its ransom, a soul asks for the truth that is its life. It asks for the love that will not cease or fail. It asks for eternal happiness. In short, it asks for God, Christ, his Head and Liberator. It asks for the company of the angels. It asks for Heaven. Being unable to set out by itself to conquer this supernatural world, given that "flesh and blood" hold it back, subject it, shackle it, entangle its will ("flesh and blood cannot inherit the kingdom of God"), this soul was claimed for Jesus by His vicar on earth. Pius IX takes up the defense of its eternal, immortal rights, ransoms it anew, frees it. Protecting it from surroundings that are harmful, contagious, and fatal to it, he places it in the mystical Eden of the Catholic, apostolic, Roman Church, where it will grow in the admirable light of the gospel.

This light will shine within this soul to make it "know you, the only true God, and Jesus Christ whom you have sent" (Jn 17:3), to make it imitate His example, to follow in His footsteps that are bathed with His precious blood—blood that the soul will one day offer on the holy altar for the sins of the world.

Pius IX knew what Baptism is. Pius IX knew what and how much a soul is worth. In order to save it he risks everything, in an evangelical manner, and therefore with the innocence of a dove but with the cunning of a serpent. He is meek and gentle as a lamb, but courageous as the Lion of Judah, when the hand of the foreigner and partisan reaches out to rescue the son of his soul, whom he has adopted in Jesus Christ and in the Church, his Mother.

Pius IX is as great as Moses on the slopes of Sinai, on whose forehead shines the terrible light of God's justice, which never compromises. Pius IX resembles more than Neptune the fierce waves of the stormy ocean on which are confounded in the whirlpool of passions the pride and the wrath of princes and kings, of the great and the insignificant who call for this soul. Pius IX responds with a firm "*Non possumus.*" Against it are hurled the arrogance of kings, the hypocritical, cunning diplomacy of all the governments and the parliaments of the world, breaking up into enormous bursts of foam.

Pius IX, in the Mortara case, recommended that the world study the most basic principles of Christian doctrine. It is clear that I am not speaking here to atheists, who admit nothing superior to matter, or to freethinkers, whether they be positivists or deists. They limit themselves to fatalism, or else they acknowledge only a God who cannot be encountered, who is hidden amid the confused pathways of an absurd, swampy fetishism. Nor am I speaking to those who profess indifferentism or to the freethinkers and rationalists who admit and respect only what reason, understood in their fashion, can create or contrive with regard to divine worship and morality.

It is clear that all supporters of systems that are so convenient for degraded, corrupt man will laugh at all that I have just written and will condemn the sequestration of the Mortara child as barbaric and despotic.

I have no other argument and defense with which to counter such sophists except the words of Dante: "Care not about them, but look and pass on."

As for the Protestants and the members of all sorts of sects who raise their voices in chorus against the Roman Church and accuse her of being intolerant and intransigent, I will only say that, if they had not become freethinkers and had not forgotten the foundations of the Faith, then in similar circumstances they could have acted only in the way in which Pius IX acted.

But instead I turn chiefly to Catholics, and immediately I come across those who are surprised and astonished because they do not know or because they have forgotten.

We refrain from giving them the title they deserve. To such Catholics I merely repeat the words of Veuillot:

The world and society have forgotten Christian doctrine: let them study it, therefore, and learn what God's rights are and those of His Church. They themselves invoke God as their Father who is in Heaven. They call the Church their Holy Mother. They will have children too. If one of them was arrested by a foreigner or by an enemy who mistreated him and embittered his life, would they not pounce like lions to save that child who is so dear to them? Let them understand, therefore, that God and the Church too, our Parents in the order of grace, have the right to snatch from Hell a child of theirs who is held in captivity in "darkness and the shadow of death".

To those proud Catholics who dare to call into question the acts of the spiritual authority and are ready to disapprove of them and to condemn them, I will say that they are Catholic in name and appearance only. The mission of the supernatural authority of the Church is to subject every intellect in respect to the Faith.

To timid, cowardly Catholics who respect the rights of the Church but do not dare to witness externally to their faith, I will say that cowardice is a very ugly thing in every order of reality, but in religious matters it is close to desertion and apostasy. Let them reflect well on this.

But I turn in particular to the half Catholics who are fainthearted and weak, fond of compromises and settlements. They are looking for deals and concessions where they are absolutely unacceptable. They dream up who knows what ideas of bringing the Church closer to what they call in their jargon "the modern spirit, the ideas of the day". They claim that the Church should adapt to their lofty, elevated criterion and adopt these ideas, or at least let them enter, reorganize, and take root within her. The half Catholics are lovers of "balancing games", as Pius IX used to say. In applying to the Mortara case their ideas and their extravagant theories about cutting deals and reaching a settlement, they cannot help opening their eyes wide, shrugging their shoulders, and raising their heads to Heaven. If ladies are the ones following these same precepts, ladies impassioned with the sweet, ethereal emotions of modern sentimentalism, which borders on sensuality, upon hearing the story of the Mortara child they tremble, their blood runs cold, their hair stands on end, and they nearly swoon. Such Catholics often go to Confession and Communion, many times the very day after having attended theatrical works or scandalous balls. They give alms to the poor, they are called "religious persons", but for all that they do not understand how Pius IX could have *snatched* a child from his parents. To their way of thinking, it was an atrocious, horrendous act: the poor child, the afflicted mother ... Look, they are already shedding tears. The result? Little less than an act of ostracism, a violent, inconsiderate anathema.

The one who is writing these lines has witnessed similar scenes many times. For these "liberal Catholics" we feel much compassion, but their astonishment does not surprise us, and their tears do not move us. With Saint Paul we will say: "We cannot do anything against the truth, but only for the truth."

These Catholics are more or less imbued or saturated with the dismal doctrines and tendencies of modern naturalism, the older brother of the liberalism condemned by the Church, the product and natural result of religious sentimentalism, which reduces everything to impressions and which can be summarized in the famous but most unfortunate maxim: "All that I like is good; all that I detest and dislike is bad." To these fainthearted, weak Catholics who look for deals, concessions, and compromises between God's rights and the demands of the world that hates Jesus Christ and is the enemy of His Cross, I will repeat the terrible words of the Apostle to the Gentiles: "What accord has Christ with Belial (or Satan)?" (2 Cor 6:15).

It is therefore useless, vain, and superfluous to look for ways out and to imagine compromises and agreements concerning the Mortara case. It is absurd to claim that God and His Church should renounce their rights and withdraw, frightened by the affliction of a family and by the tears of a mother. After having tried means of persuasion, Pius IX had no other solution left but the very painful but indispensable one of separating Edgardo from his parents. Given that they did not consent, Pius IX had to proceed, as Pope and as King, to the order of sequestration.

This is what the natural law teaches; this is what divine law sanctions and confirms; this is what the gospel proclaims and what the ecclesiastical canons have always commanded and prescribed. "Dura lex, sed tamen lex" (The law is hard, but nevertheless it is the law). This is precisely the case in which to apply in its full force the decisive aphorism of all jurisprudence.

And now, in conclusion, we challenge a whole series of persons: all who hypocritically and pharisaically are moved with compassion by the lot of the Mortara child and of his afflicted parents; all who looked or look with astonishment and surprise, or with frowns and sadness, or with displeasure and indignation, or with rancor and hatred, at the Mortara case; all who disapprove of the noble, magnanimous action of Pius IX, whether they be unbelievers, Protestants, atheists, rationalists, positivists, materialists, radicals, republicans, Freemasons, or persons affiliated or associated with Freemasonry, that eternal, implacable enemy of Jesus Christ and of the papacy. To all of them in mass we say: lift up your eyes and see. There you will see Alexander II, the Russian emperor, who sends into exile thousands of Polish Catholics to the horrendous cold in icy Siberia, snatching away from parents, siblings, and wives their sons, brothers, and husbands, and leaving them to die without pity or mercy in the most profound and terrible poverty. Meanwhile the great Pius IX, from the Vatican Hill, uttered an eloquent, sublime cry from the depth of his sorrow: "The world attacked me with fury for having saved the Mortara child by separating him from his parents, and the Russian emperor takes thousands of souls away from me, the common Father of the faithful!"

All you who have condemned or now condemn Pius IX, reflect on what the rationalist governments and their leaders have done and are doing today in the name of progress and liberty. These representatives of the atheistic state—that is, the despotic, tyrannical, barbarous state—devise in their tumultuous meetings and then mercilessly apply perverse laws that attack the most sacred rights of conscience. Their teaching, a teaching that is antireligious and preeminently Masonic, is centralized and monopolized in pestilential professorships held by men without faith, without principles, and without morality. Parents are obliged to hand over the dear beloved souls of their sons to these demons in the flesh so that they might corrupt them and drag them with them into the abyss of Hell. Otherwise, these sons will have no career, no civil rights, sometimes not even a roof over their heads.

Observe what Freemasonry does: It enchants many poor young men who are deceived and blinded, eager for novelty, occultism, and mysteries. After attracting them with these baits, it turns them into perjurers, barbarians who are cruel to their parents, brothers, and friends, friends in whose hearts they one day will have to plunge the dagger of this bloodthirsty god that the Lodges are, if that were necessary so as not to break the oath to keep the secret to which a Freemason sacrifices everything. The Freemason sacrifices to this secret his possessions, his life, his parents, his family, religion, morality, the Church, and Jesus Christ (whom he must hate if he wants to be a good brother).

Observe what freethinkers of all stripes have done and are doing. They have despoiled the clergy, confiscating the sacred treasures of the Church, profaning the monasteries, expelling the monks and the nuns and staining with their blood the streets and the squares of the cities in rebellion, to the strains of "La Marseillaise". Recall the September massacres, the 1870 Revolution, the Commune of Paris, the soldiers of Garibaldi in Italy. And then accuse Pius IX, condemn Pius IX, call *him* a despot and a barbarian because he separated a child from his parents so as to save his soul, to make him a brother of Jesus Christ, a friend of the angels, and an heir of Heaven.

Ah! Amid your cackling, in the middle of the whirlpool of your hatreds and resentments, over the thick cloud and the dense fogs of your ignorance and pride, high above the movement of the base, treacherous passions that the infernal Serpent awakens and provokes in your ignoble hearts, arises, ascends and towers, like a new Moses on Sinai, at the summit of the Vatican, the great, admirable, immortal Pontiff of the Immaculate and of the *Syllabus*. The flash of his glance, together with the thunder of his sublime "*Non possumus*", silences your "Tolle, tolle, crucifige eum" (Away with him, away with him, crucify him) (Jn 19:15) and leaves Pius IX on a throne that is still great, still noble, and unvanquished.

The controversy over the Mortara child was only a pretext. What they wanted was to humiliate the Church by discrediting the papacy, so as to put an end to it with its temporal power. The outcome thereof, however, is what Horace wrote: "Parturient montes, nascetur ridiculus mus" (The mountains will labor to bring forth, but only a ridiculous little mouse will be born.)

The accusers of Pius IX, like those of Jesus, of whom he is the visible vicar, are squashed under the weight of their inconsistent, ridiculous calumnies. Today, beside the great Pontiff of the Immaculate and of the *Syllabus*, is raised the voice of that same child of yore, now a man, a priest, and a religious, a son of Saint Augustine. He brandishes the sword of the word and defends Pius IX, his guardian angel, his Father and Protector, to whom, after God, he owes everything.

Let this last word that Don Pio has just pronounced be a modest flower placed on the tomb that encloses the revered remains of Pius IX, which were persecuted and profaned by modern Freemasonry. May this flower remain there without spoiling or fading, as the homage of a most faithful heart and of the profoundest filial gratitude.

There will come a day, yes, and it is not far away, in which, once they have stopped listening to the calumnies and the "*Crucifige*" (shouts of "Crucify!") of the dregs of humanity, posterity will accept the poor arguments of the Mortara child, so as to tie them into scented garlands of immortal flowers that will adorn and decorate the altar on which the Catholic world will greet, with enthusiastic acclamations, PIUS IX, THE SAINT.